STOPPING SCHOOL VIOLENCE

An Essential Guide

Special Report

Preface by Kenneth S. Trump, M.P.A.,
Consulting Editor

Health & Administration Development Group
ASPEN PUBLISHERS, INC.

"This publication is designed to provide accurate and authoritative information in regard to the subject matter covered. It is sold with the understanding that the publisher is not engaged in rendering legal, accounting, or other professional services. If legal advice or other professional assistance is required, the services of a competent professional person should be sought."

— From a Declaration of Principles jointly adopted by a Committee of the American Bar Association and a Committee of Publishers and Associates.

Copyright © 1999
by
Aspen Publishers, Inc.
A Wolters Kluwer Company
200 Orchard Ridge Drive
Gaithersburg, MD 20878

ISBN: 0-8342-1716-3

About Aspen Publishers

For more than 35 years, Aspen has been a leading professional publisher in a variety of disciplines. Aspen's vast information resources are available in both print and electronic formats. We are committed to providing the highest quality information available in the most appropriate format for our customers.

Visit Aspen's Internet site for more information resources, directories, articles, and a searchable version of Aspen's full catalog, including the most recent publications: **http://www.aspenpublishers.com**

To order a catalog of Aspen publications, call 800/234-1660.

Printed in the United States of America

Contents

Preface

Introduction

Part I. Prevention

Security Safeguards

ASSESSING AND MAINTAINING SECURITY

PREVENTION OF VIOLENCE

Student Behavior: The Warning Signs

RED FLAGS

CULTS AND GANGS

Part II. Crisis Management

CRISIS PROCEDURES

RESPONDING TO WEAPONS

Part III. Legal Issues, Policies, and Procedures

Part IV. Internet and WWW Guide

Part V. Financial Support

Reprints Available

For Bulk Discounts:
   Discounts are available for bulk quantity purchases of this publication. Please contact Linda McKenna at 301/417-7591 or by e-mail at lmckenna@aspenpubl.com.

For Multiple Quantity Reprints:
   Article reprints are available in quantities of 100 or more. We can customize your reprints specifically for your school or district. Please contact Linda McKenna at 301/417-7591 or by e-mail at lmckenna@aspenpubl.com.

   Visit Aspen's Internet site for more information resources, directories, articles, and a searchable version of Aspen's full catalog, including the most recent publications:
   http://www.aspenpublishers.com

Preface

A s consulting editor and long-term contributor to Aspen's *Inside School Safety* newsletter, I view the safety challenges facing school officials and members of their school communities with mixed emotions. On one hand, I wish that there was no need for school security newsletters, consultants, and related specialty resources. On the other hand, I recognize that we unfortunately live in a society where these resources are increasingly needed and, most important, where *quality* resources are relatively scarce.

It is therefore with pleasure that one of my first acts as the new consulting editor is to introduce this special report of resources on some of the most pressing issues, questions, and information needs of interest to individuals tasked with improving their school safety and security. This guide is a compilation of safe schools materials developed into one resource to meet these needs. Administrators, teachers, support staff, and other individuals have access here to the insights on a wide range of hot topics from numerous leaders in the professional field of school safety.

A comprehensive approach to school safety includes a balance of education, prevention, intervention, discipline, security, and crisis preparedness measures. This guide offers tips on various aspects in these categories. While there is no single strategy or "silver bullet" for fixing the ills of our society, and in turn our schools, it is comforting to know that there are some practical and realistic steps that can be taken to reduce the risks of violence taking place in or around our schools.

Following a thoughtful look at what should be learned from the latest high-profile school violence incident in our nation, **Part One** of the guide begins by addressing security safeguard measures in our schools. Specific items touched upon include assessing security, the use of selected equipment and staffing options, recognizing bombs and weapons, and the use of anonymous hotlines. It also touches upon some of the underlying issues behind the violence we see in schools, including anger management, student threat assessment, early warning signs of potential violent behavior, recognizing gang and cult presence on campus, and related tips for preventing and managing youth-related conflict.

Part Two takes readers beyond the prevention measures by recognizing that, unfortunately, we must be prepared to manage those incidents that we cannot prevent. While this may sound pessimistic to some, if we have learned anything from the national school violence tragedies of recent years, it is that we must be prepared for a crisis. Knowing how to distinguish crimes from disruptive behaviors, having procedures in place for various staff to take in an emergency, and knowing how to handle weapons and bombs clearly will take us in the right direction for successful management of related incidents. The undesired reality of being a school official in today's society is that we must not only anticipate some events, but we must also be prepared for the worst. One colleague put it best by saying that, "I would rather apologize for being prepared than apologize for having done nothing." Readers will learn how to deal with parents in the aftermath of crisis with a sample written notice provided in this section.

One of the big pieces of the "How?" question involves the legal community. Unfortunately for our educators, they now need to have a solid foundation of knowledge about the legal decisions that impact their abilities to function in a safe school environment. **Part Three** covers a broad range of topics ranging from FERPA to policies and procedures associated with safe schools planning.

Parts Four and **Five** help school officials "close the loop" in their questions by providing pointers to online resources, grants and related funding, and professional resource organizations that work with school safety on a regular basis. Understanding what the security threats are today, developing prevention and intervention plans, and knowing legal boundaries are important. Knowing where to get the resources for implementing programs and strategies related to these components now offers the next, and sometimes often missed, step of identifying resources for doing so.

The threats to safe schools have changed over the years and are likely to continue to do so. We cannot afford to continue sending our school officials to work without the training, guidelines, and resources to prevent and manage violence. The pages that follow, as well as future Aspen publications on school safety, will make sure that such resources are available.

Any publication is only good if its readers put to use the information given to them. Take this guide, digest the information, and communicate regularly with members of your school community about school safety. While we cannot prevent every tragedy, we owe it to the students, staff, and parents to reduce school security risks and to prepare for effectively managing critical incidents.

—Kenneth S. Trump, M.P.A.

Kenneth S. Trump, M.P.A.

Kenneth S. Trump is president and CEO of National School Safety and Security Services, a Cleveland-based national consulting firm specializing in school security and crisis preparedness training, assessments, and related consulting services. He served over seven years with the Division of Safety and Security for the Cleveland Public Schools, the last three as founding supervisor of its Youth Gang Unit. Ken then served as assistant director of a federal-funded gang project in three southwest Cleveland suburbs, where he was also director of security for the ninth largest Ohio public school system. In 1997, he expanded his training and consulting service into a full-time operation, which has included work with schools and law enforcement officials in 30 states.

Ken currently chairs the K-12 Security Subcommittee of the Educational Institutions Security Standing Committee of the American Society for Industrial Security. He is co-founder and served eight years as vice president of the Midwest Gang Investigators Association's Ohio Chapter, and is also a member of the International Association of Professional Security Consultants. He is quoted extensively on school security and crisis preparedness issues, including on "Good Morning America," "ABC World News Tonight," "NBC Nightly News," MSNBC, CNBC, "CNN Headline News," "Fox News," "The Gayle King Show," and in The Associated Press. In May of 1999, Ken provided testimony on school safety at a hearing of the U.S. Senate Committee on Health, Education, Labor, and Pensions.

In addition to his graduate degree in public administration and an undergraduate degree in social service, Ken has extensive specialized training in his field. He serves as the consulting editor to Aspen's *Inside School Safety* newsletter. More information on Ken and his firm is available at Web site ***www.schoolsecurity.org.***

Introduction

We Must Learn from the Tragedy in Littleton

How should schools respond to their students' concerns in the aftermath of a tragic school shooting like Littleton?

Once again, Americans watched in horror as the facts unfolded and young killers took to the halls of their school with deadly weapons, bent on murdering their fellow students.

The April 20, 1999, mass killing in Littleton, Colo., however, was different from earlier school shootings. With 15 dead, it set a record.

Once again we are asking ourselves how such horrific tragedies can be prevented in the future.

"Everyone's searching for the magic sound bite, the answer to it all," says Marsha Hubbard, safe schools specialist in the Virginia Department of Education's Office of Special Education and Student Services, in Richmond. "But unfortunately, there isn't one," she says.

"However, there are many things school administrators — and others — can do to help prevent future school killings," she says.

Improve Student-Adult Communication

Interviews with Columbine High School students reveal that many students had heard comments by the two shooters, to the effect that they would one day commit violent acts at school. Yet students did not come forward to tell responsible adults or police what they had heard.

Many schools have responded to students' reluctance to share important safety information by encouraging anonymous reporting or by offering cash rewards that lead to the recovery of a firearm on school grounds or on a student.

"No code of silence among students is worth the life of friends or classmates," stressed Eugene Lewis, chief of police for the Galveston Independent School District, when he urged district principals to remind students of the district's Crime Stoppers anonymous reporting program.

More than 500 schools around the country are opening up communication lines between students and adults through Youth Crime Watch. "This program that emphasizes peer reporting and student-adult communication, reduces school violence by empowering students to work with each other and with adults to keep their schools safe," says Terrence Modglin, executive director of the Miami-based national nonprofit.

"We need to listen to kids!" stresses Hubbard. In spite of their busy schedules, administrators and teachers must take the time to listen to any student who has something to report — and follow up the listening with investigation. One reason so many students do not come forward with critical safety information is that they do not believe an adult will really listen or take what they have to say seriously, many school safety experts believe.

Follow Up on Threats

"Adults must follow up on safety threats, student tips, and teacher referrals," insists Lewis. "It's time-consuming because a huge number of students make threats. But we have to do it," he says. Prior to the Littleton shooting, Lewis's district had already increased the staff time available for such investigations. And parents are always notified when their child has made a threat, Lewis says.

"In the cases that seem to have the greatest potential for danger, we seek parental permission to search the student's room," Lewis says. He adds that while many parents believe their child could never commit a violent crime, "they are generally cooperative." Lewis's department takes the threat of school violence seriously enough that it is planning to begin filing criminal charges against students who threaten violence at school.

Prepare Teachers and Administrators

Some people believe an effective way to prevent school violence is to arm teachers. In fact, when the April 20 tragedy took place, a measure to make it easier for Coloradans to carry concealed weapons had passed the Colorado Senate. The bill was scheduled to go before a House panel the next day, but its sponsor pulled it. According to the Rocky Mountain Gun Owners, the measure would allow teachers to protect themselves and their classrooms.

"The proposal is ludicrous!" says Hubbard. "Arming teachers would simply mean putting firearms in the hands of people who don't know how to use them. And that certainly wouldn't make schools safer," she argues. Lewis agrees. "Any legislator who thinks it's a good idea hasn't given serious thought to the subject of school safety," says Lewis, who adds that his officers spend a great deal of time mediating between teachers and students. He is not eager to insert guns into such situations.

Set Behavior Standards for All

"Athletes should be held to the same standards of conduct as all other students," says Peter Blauvelt, president of the National Alliance for Safe Schools, based in College Park, Md. Blauvelt says that some school administrators use athletes to intimidate students who "act up." "Frequently, athletes tease, bully, and humiliate other students," he says, which may explain why Eric Harris and Dylan Klebold aimed much of their fire at boys wearing caps. And while no one can excuse Klebold's and Harris's actions, the boys fit the profile of many students who kill: ridiculed, rejected, and socially isolated.

"Schools should not neglect to address the everyday bad behavior, like bullying, harassing, pushing, and shoving. Don't wait until guns are involved," says Hubbard. She believes one of schools' main missions is to teach appropriate behavior.

Incidentally, behavior has improved at Thurston High School in Springfield, Ore., where a student killed two others in May 1998, according to Principal Larry Bentz. Bentz reports that, since last year's shootings, his school has seen fewer fights, less bullying, less harassment, and much kinder behavior in general. "There is a silver lining to the tragedy," he says. "The students have really learned the importance of treating others with respect."

Behavior should include attire, according to Hubbard. "And it is entirely appropriate for schools to ban 'Gothic' clothing." Students, just like adults, she says, should know that certain clothing is inappropriate for school or work. "During leisure time, students may dress as they wish," she says. But will the ban on trench coats, adopted by Denver schools since the Littleton slayings, help prevent school violence? "That's for the psychologists to say," Hubbard replies.

Kenneth Trump, executive director of National School and Safety Security Services, in Cleveland, favors school uniforms and dress codes. But he is not optimistic that banning trench coats will actually do much to stop school violence.

Provide Help for Troubled Students

Much more counseling and mental health services are needed at our schools, says Trump. "Situations where there's one counselor for 400 kids or where one psychologist has to cover many schools in a district are not meeting students' needs," he says. "And a great many students are hurting," adds Hubbard. She recommends that school districts make the provision of mental health services to students a high priority.

Call for School Safety Training of Teachers and Administrators

While many school districts offer inservice training to teachers on school safety issues, "the agenda may be so full that safety training can easily fall to the bottom of the list," Hubbard says. She recommends, instead, that education in early warning signs of violence, prevention techniques, anger management, and conflict management be included in college teacher education programs and in degree programs for school administrators as well.

Teachers need to be much more prepared, Hubbard says. School officials can help bring about such additions to teacher education programs by stressing to those who run them the importance of school safety training for all certified teachers.

Monitor the Internet

Last summer, Hubbard recalls, many school safety experts stressed the need for school officials to be on high alert to Internet web sites containing information on making bombs. In light of Klebold's and Harris's ability to make explosives, presumably obtained through the Internet, such monitoring may make sense. But it is not easy to do. Most schools, which presumably already have Internet use policies in place, should stress to students the importance of such policies and should remind parents to monitor their children's Internet use at home.

Schools Can't Do It All

Of course, schools alone cannot solve the problem of school violence. Schools should not hesitate to ask for help from parents, local residents, business leaders, and students. Schools reflect the community, and vice versa, says Trump. And there is a role to play for everyone in the community in making sure our schools stay safe.

—Inside School Safety Editor, April Moore

Part I

Prevention

Security Safeguards

Student Behavior: The Warning Signs

Security Safeguards
ASSESSING AND MAINTAINING SECURITY

Addressing Violence: Recommendations from Those Who Have Been There

New Resource Outlines the Practical Lessons of Pearl, Paducah, Jonesboro, and Springfield

School safety officials now have access to a resource designed to help prevent and react to violence, thanks to a brainstorming session among parties most involved with the spate of recent school shootings.

In June 1998, 58 school administrators, law enforcement representatives, emergency medical workers, mayors, ministers, and others from Paducah, Ky.; Pearl, Miss.; Jonesboro, Ark.; and Springfield, Ore., gathered at a Memphis hotel to compare notes. It was facilitated by Iowa-based school safety expert Dr. Bill Reisman.

Techniques to Prevent Violence

Conference attendees developed the following recommendations for school administrators to prevent school violence:

1. Organize a meeting to educate parents about signs that could indicate their child is moving toward destructive behavior. "I've worked with families where kids' bedrooms were filled with posters depicting violence, where kids were even sleeping in coffins," says Reisman. "And the parents had not a clue."

When parents know what to look for, they can intervene more effectively.

2. Hold a meeting regarding each student when he or she is promoted to the next grade level. The meeting should include both the teacher of the grade being completed and the teacher for the following year. The student and his or her parents should also attend.

This meeting is an excellent opportunity for the new teacher and the student to get acquainted and for the new teacher to benefit from the previous teacher's insights about the student's behavior, toward both himself and others. The upcoming teacher can make sure the student and parents understand expectations for the next grade. Students and parents can also ask questions and provide information.

Conference participants recommended that these meetings be held, at a minimum, for students who appear troubled. Preferably they should be held for all students.

3. Ask teachers to watch for signs that a student may be about to engage in destructive behavior. The school counselor should be at the hub of this effort, says Reisman. Homeroom teachers should be on the alert for bizarre clothing. English teachers should watch for dark themes, such as death and violence, in students' writing. History teachers should take note of fascination with Hitler, infamous cults, or the occult. Art teachers should keep an eye out for dark themes in artistic creations. Physical education teachers should be alert to signs of self-mutilation.

When teachers observe any of these signs, it should be reported to the counselor. The counselor can then assess if a student exhibits troubling behavior in several classes, or whether a teacher's report is an

Can Pistol-Packing Teachers Deter School Shootings?

Teachers should be given firearms training and carry guns to prevent school violence, a University of Chicago academic says.

John Lott, who recently concluded a study of U.S. crime statistics, says "visible deterrence" is the best deterrence in the classroom.

Having a couple of administrators or teachers carry guns on campus would be an inexpensive way to "increase the deputized police force," he said.

The police can't be every place all the time, Lott said, and there can be a "very long period of time between when a person starts to fire and when the police are able to arrive at the scene."

Lott is a fellow at the university's law school.

His suggestion recently was rejected by Arkansas Republican Gov. Mike Huckabee, who said giving guns to teachers would mean "going back to the Wild West."

Lott's "More Guns, Less Crime: Understanding Crime and Gun Control Laws" is $22.95 and is available in many commercial book stores.

isolated incident — which suggests violence is far less likely. Making the best use of teachers' observations, Reisman explains, lies in having someone at the hub, someone who can bring all the pieces together.

4. Limit students' access to the building before school to 15 minutes prior to the first class.

5. Refer any student caught with a weapon on school grounds to an inpatient psychiatric facility for a 72-hour psychiatric evaluation.

6. Remove all lockers. So that students will not have to carry their textbooks with them at all times, issue students two copies of each book. To defray the doubled textbook cost, approach businesses and community organizations to help with the expense. Other options include hefty end-of-the-year fines for disfigured or damaged books and sale of existing lockers.

An anteroom would be designated for students' coats and other items traditionally stored in lockers.

7. Require students who bring their lunch to school to bring it in a see-through plastic bag.

8. Install fire alarms that leave finger prints when set off. Educate all students about the new feature for a deterrant effect. When asked if the technology now exists for such equipment, Reisman said that if it does not, it could easily be developed.

9. Require all school employees to wear photo identification badges at all times.

10. Equip bus drivers with hand-held metal detectors and a means to engage in continuous voice contact with police and school administrators. Since a video camera on a school bus does little to prevent violence, schools should seek parent volunteers to ride buses and monitor student behavior.

Reacting to Crisis (see also page 64, "Responding to Weapons")

Participants recommend that schools take the following steps to prepare themselves in the event that violence erupts:

1. Establish procedures for notifying teachers of crises so they can protect students. A code sentence over the public address system is recommended. For example, "Would Mr. Wilson please come to the office?" could alert teachers to lock their doors, pull down all shades, and instruct students to lie on the floor. Teachers with students in the gym, cafeteria, or other non-classroom sites should proceed to the nearest classroom. Teachers should remain in this mode until signaled by the principal that the crisis is over.

2. Name two or three administrators as leaders in the event of violence. Each of these people should have a brightly colored vest, building keys, and a map of the school floor plan. Notify police and emergency medical personnel that, in the event of an emergency, all their questions should be directed to the individuals wearing the vests.

3. Sponsor a beginning-of-the-year in-service session. Include police, fire, emergency medical personnel, and all others who may be needed in a violent crisis. Discuss and clarify all parties' roles.

4. Designate an off-site building where worried parents and others can gather for news about their children and the situation. A large church, civic center, movie theater, or other building would suffice. Notify parents and the press of its purpose and location. Meeting attendees noted that during crises, nearby roads were so clogged with frantic parents, reporters, and onlookers that people abandoned their vehicles as far as two miles from the school and traveled the rest of the way on foot.

5. Train teachers and staff in basic First Aid. Participants said that school officials were hampered by the unevenness of training. "For example, there might be several school staff members who knew CPR and mouth-to-mouth resuscitation, but none who knew how to stop bleeding," says Reisman.

6. Use community mental health resources. Develop a list of approved counselors who will work with students and staff following violent incidents.

7. Coordinate two-way radio communication with police, fire, emergency medical, and other personnel. Be sure that everyone speaks the same language. Too often, communication is stymied by professional code. Says Reisman, "The announcement of a '12-15' is not likely to tell a school administrator anything." Participants recommended that everyone using two-way radio communication during a school emergency avoid all coded terms.

8. Prepare for the media onslaught. Deal with the press in a way that keeps reporters from overwhelming school and emergency personnel but that satifies their need for information. Have a prepared press release to distribute in the event of a crisis, describing how information will be disseminated — including the site of press conferences and their times. "Do not deviate from this pre-established press plan," stresses Reisman. Pre-set press meetings help separate confirmed fact from rumor.

9. Declare the entire school property part of the crime scene. Keeping the press at bay is extremely important, said participants, because reporters in some instances interviewed students whose names were nationally broadcast. With this information public, students could become the victims of pedophiles who, thanks to the news interview, know how to reach the students.

10. Ensure that a mechanism exists for obtaining the day's attendance roster. Such information is key in accounting for all students on the day of a crisis.

11. Include hospital-type identification bracelets and indelible markers in First Aid kits. In the pandemonium surrounding school violence, victim identification was often done crudely, by writing with pens on arms and clothing.

12. Stipulate in school emergency policy that any ambulance carrying injured students includes a teacher who knows the students.

Also require that teachers maintain a copy of the most recent yearbook in their classroom and that they bring it to the hospital in case further identification is necessary.

—April Moore

Managing Safety on Large Campuses

Simple Strategies Can Reduce Security, Faculty Worries

No matter how hard they try, school resource officers assigned to large and/or multi-building campuses cannot be everywhere or solve every problem. Environmental challenges — large crowds of students, openness to trespassers, and basic mobility and navigation issues — unfairly limit their effectiveness.

Two schools with several large campuses have adopted the following strategies to overcome such challenges:

College Students Aid Security

Because only one or two resource officers are typically assigned to a school, their visibility on campus can be limited.

Operations Manager Jim Stark provides extra staffing during the busiest times of the school day by hiring college students as security aides at several schools in the San Diego Unified School District Police Department.

Hiring additional security for busy times of the school day, such as lunch and when school lets out, provides additional eyes to spot problems, says Stark.

"We try to have two to four security aides around early in the morning, during the noon hour, and in the afternoon to watch for people who don't belong in the halls or on the grounds," he says. "We don't want these aides to be part of a confrontation, however. We want them to be the eyes and ears for the police officer and the school."

Stark says college students are recruited to work part-time as security aides. The school district publicizes the jobs at local colleges and universities.

The students earn approximately $8 per hour for shifts of 3 to 4 hours. The pay and the ability to work around class schedules has created a sizable pool of interested aides who are eager to work in the jobs. Recruiting education majors or students with an interest in a law enforcement career can also provide the students with experience for their future careers.

Simple Technique Makes Security a "Lock"

Many teachers and administrators share concerns about being caught off guard — and alone — by unexpected and sometimes unwelcome visitors, such as an angry parent who moves unnoticed through empty hallways.

Stark recommends that teachers keep the door to their classroom locked when they are alone before or after school, or during times when the school is largely deserted. This prevents parents or other unauthorized visitors from catching them off guard or putting them in danger.

Stark also recommends that teachers lock their classroom doors as soon as their students are in the classroom and class begins. "If anyone wants to get in, they can knock and be seen before entering the classroom. This is especially good if there's a problem with a parent. It keeps people from wandering in and creating a scene in front of the class."

If a parent shows up outside the door and appears angry, the teacher can step out or call the office for assistance without exposing students to a confrontation in the classroom.

Bike Patrols on Large Campuses

The Clark County School District in Las Vegas, Nev., adapted an idea that works well for metro police forces in warm environments. It uses bicycles to provide an efficient link for school police officers who need to patrol large campuses.

The bicycle patrols have proven a benefit for getting around on large school campuses, including one school campus that covers about 3.5 acres. Bicycles permit officers to increase response times and navigate crowds of students when a fight or other campus problem arises.

The bicycle program has also proven a benefit to other middle and elementary schools in the area of the high schools. Instead of using a

Clinton: 10 Percent Of U.S. Schools Face Serious Crime

One in 10 American public schools were confronted with serious violence — such as rape and robbery — during the 1996-97 school year, the White House said in its first-ever survey on school violence.

The report also found that 43 percent of schools reported no crime at all. Overall, about 1,000 crimes per 100,000 students were reported.

Schools, for the most part, remain a safe haven from serious crime, but President Clinton said tougher safety standards are imperative.

Many students still face a "far more frightening reality every time they walk through the school door," Clinton said at a White House ceremony announcing the Education Department's results.

The Education Department report is the result of a survey of 1,234 public elementary, middle and secondary schools in all 50 states.

"Violence and Discipline Problems in U.S. Public Schools: 1996-1997" is free from the National Library of Education, 555 New Jersey Ave., NW, Room 101, Washington, DC 20208, 877/433-7827 or 202/205-5019; Internet, http://nces.ed.gov.

vehicle, officers can ride their bikes and arrive more quickly to many locations.

"The bikes make short trips much quicker, especially when the beat patrol people from the high schools can cut through alleys and across fields to reach area elementary schools," says Dan Reyes, chief of school police.

The Clark County School District received a $30,000 grant from the Hughes Corporation to purchase 36 bicycles for campus officers.

School Violence Prevention Is Attainable, Experts Say

R outine analysis of student infractions is one tool school administrators can use to prevent school violence, experts said during a veritable "how-to" teleconference on the subject.

Robert Michela, co-developer of "Safe Schools: A Handbook for Practitioners," demonstrated how to fill out the incident reports, which record violent and minor infractions at a school, and the consistency of those infractions.

Administrators should then determine risk-reduction objectives for each potential security problem. The objectives should be "realistic and easy to implement," said Michela, deputy director of the Reston, Va.-based DynMeridian security company.

'You can't effectively manage a crisis while trying to give CPR to someone on the bathroom floor. Let rescue professionals or staff handle that responsibility.'
—Peter Blauvelt, president, National Alliance for Safe Schools

---

The National Association of Secondary School Principals (NASSP) sponsored the interactive school violence teleconference with violence control experts and national educators that was broadcast via satellite to 47 sites.

Roughly 200 participants were able to e-mail questions to — and view presentations from — a panel of three experts on topics ranging from how to handle a school crisis situation to tools and methodology on putting together a comprehensive security plan.

Define a Security Plan

Michela outlined a five-step security plan that uses tools to identify the current climate of violence in a school and determine risk-reduction objectives.

As an early prevention method, school administrators should survey students and staff on their school's safety level. Michela said "students are the key. Get them involved. They like to do things to improve their school."

Violence prevention must take place before high school "when kids are already at risk," said Stephen Sroka, a former K-12 teacher and principal and president of the Cleveland-based Health Education Consultants.

School administrators should be aware of several traits in students that can be manifestations of mental problems.

For example, students who mutilate their bodies by cutting or burning themselves, an increasingly common sight among some school-age children, generally are depressed, Sroka said. He added that the most common weapon in schools today isn't a knife or gun, but an inexpensive "box cutter" that's easily hidden and often metal detector-proof.

Kids who often show signs of depression, especially those with clinical depression, have a much higher chance of becoming violent, Sroka said.

Four Time Zones to a Crisis

A proactive school safety plan separates a crisis situation into four time zones: The first 10 minutes, the next 50 minutes, the rest of that day and subsequent days, said Peter Blauvelt, president of the National Alliance for Safe Schools.

During the first 10 minutes of a "Code Red" scene, it's crucial for administrators to stay in the main office and avoid the crime scene.

"You can't effectively manage a crisis while trying to give CPR to someone on the bathroom floor," Blauvelt said. Let rescue professionals or staff handle that responsibility, he added.

Most importantly, crisis plans need to be "practiced, practiced, practiced," he said.

An inexpensive prevention tactic, Blauvelt added, is to determine the major issues affecting individual schools by breaking up student referral reports into generic files, such as files for disruption, fighting, alcohol, arson, and cheating. Most schools already have this data.

And Blauvelt criticized zero-tolerance policies, which he said equate to "zero options" for students. School administrators instead should develop resources that "deal with situations as they play out," he said.

Anne Kauffman, a Fairfax County, Va., middle school teacher who participated at the teleconference's Washington, D.C., site, said, "It was good to hear what [the experts'] insights were and what to look for" in potentially violent students.

For more information, contact the National Association of Secondary School Principals, 1904 Association Dr., Reston, VA 22091, 703/860-0200; Internet, http://www.nassp.org.

School Crime Assessment Tool

1. Has your community crime rate increased over the past 12 months?
2. Are more than 15 percent of your work order repairs vandalism-related?
3. Do you have an open campus?
4. Has there been an emergence of an underground student newspaper?
5. Is your community transiency rate increasing?
6. Do you have an increasing presence of graffiti in your community?
7. Do you have an increasing presence of gangs in your community?
8. Is your truancy rate increasing?
9. Are your suspension and expulsion rates increasing?
10. Have you had increased conflicts relative to dress styles, food services, and types of music played at special events?
11. Do you have an increasing number of students on probation at your school?
12. Have you had isolated racial fights?
13. Have you reduced the number of extracurricular programs and sports at your school?
14. Has there been an increasing incidence of parents withdrawing students from your school because of fear?
15. Has your budget for professional development opportunities and in-service training for your staff been reduced or eliminated?
16. Are you discovering more weapons on your campus?
17. Do you lack written screening and selection guidelines for new

teachers and other youth-serving professionals who work in your school?

18. Are drugs easily available in or around your school?
19. Are more than 40 percent of your students bused to school without the option of choice?
20. Have you had a student demonstration or other signs of unrest within the past 12 months?

Scoring and Interpretation

Multiply each affirmative answer by 5 and add the total. Scores of 0 to 20 indicate that there is not a significant school safety problem at your school. If you have scores ranging from 25 to 45, you have an emerging school safety problem and should develop a safe school plan. Scores of 50 to 70 indicate that there is a significant potential for school safety problems. A safe school plan should be a top priority. If your score is more than 70, you are sitting on a ticking time bomb. Begin working on your safe school plan immediately. Get some outside help.

Source: Ronald D. Stephens, National School Safety Center, 141 Duesenbury Drive, Suite 11, Westlake Village, CA, 91362, 805-373-9977, (F) 805-373-9277 http://www.nssc1.org.

Halt — Who Goes There?

High-tech, High-ticket ID Systems Target Trespassers

Many school administrators are finding it more and more challenging to keep track of the students — not to mention the transient workers, volunteers, and substitute teachers — in the building. And how can you distinguish the trespasser from the person with a legitimate reason to be there?

The traditional requirement that visitors register in the school office on entering the building has come to appear painfully inadequate. School officials are looking for a reliable way to maintain the integrity of their campuses.

In the Prince George's County, Md., School System, outside Washington, D.C., more than 122,000 students annually attend schools each year. Every fall, individual high schools welcome as many as 900 incoming freshman in addition to transfer students. Safety officers were concerned about the perception that students could not be recognized. "The more you know, the more control you have," says Ed Reed, assistant security director.

To make sure that the schools remained safe for students and staff, officials turned to a security arrangement that is in place in government offices and private businesses around the county — a photo ID system.

Hampering the Hallwalker...

Here are some suggestions from Peter D. Blauvelt, president of the National Alliance for Safe Schools, for dealing with hallwalkers:

Color-Coded Hallpasses

Try creating two hallpasses out of 9- by 12-inch pieces of bright-colored cardboard for each classroom. Label the cards with the classroom number. These become the hallpass — and only two students can be out at any one time. You can even color-code the hallpass for appropriate floors or wings of the school; the passing staff member will know that only particular cards should be used in certain areas of the building.

Hall Sweeps

Conduct random hall sweeps without prior announcement. Advise your teachers that if any of their students are picked up in a hall sweep and the student is without the proper hall pass, they are going to be held accountable for allowing the student to be out of class.

Teacher Peer Pressure

Another strategy that has been used with some success is when a student is found out of class, the student is placed in the nearest classroom for the remainder of the period. It doesn't take long for the recipients of these unwanted students to let the offending teachers know exactly how they feel about having their classes disrupted. Be prepared to act as mediator, as discussions can become quite heated in the faculty lounge.

The National Alliance for Safe Schools is a nonprofit corporation dedicated to making schools safe for children and staff. It's phone number is 301/306-0200.

"It was expensive, very expensive," says Reed. "But the bottom line is, it works."

The laminated ID cards resemble state driver's licenses and bear a recent photo as well as a bar code. Students and staff at all high schools must carry the ID at all times, and temporary IDs are provided to visitors. Students (but not staff) must wear their IDs on beaded nonmetallic necklaces so they are visible but do not present a choking hazard. School activity clubs raise funds by designing and selling the beaded necklaces.

"We thought about requiring the IDs in middle schools also," says Reed. "But we were concerned about the expense, and about whether younger kids had the maturity to hold onto the IDs without losing them."

School Board Mandate

The School Board incorporated the requirement that students wear their IDs into the Student Code of Conduct. Temporary IDs are provided to students who do not bring theirs to school, but refusal to wear the ID — or continued forgetting of the ID — can result in suspension.

"This system allows Investigator Counselors (school security officers) to address more students by name. And as a result, more students think they should behave,"observes Reed. "It's not 'Hey You!' but 'Hey Mary Jane!' that gets a student's attention."

Computer-based system provides many options for IDs

The ID system is a computer-based program with software that can be customized for each school's needs. Ken Maxwell, educational services administrator for Northwestern High School and all of its feeder schools, uses the system to compile a database with student background information, classroom data, and pictures. The cards are used to monitor attendance and permit event access, and the database can be accessed by school staff at any time.

"For example," says Maxwell, "If a teacher says that he is sending John Doe to the office, we can check the photo database to make sure that is who shows up."

"The goal is to make the ID a tool that students need to function in the school environment," says Maxwell.

Student pictures are printed on backgrounds that give information about the student's status — different colors represent the year in school and participation in a work study program. A light-pen is run over the bar code when a student is late for school; the computer then prints the tardy slip.

Not all school ID systems are as elaborate as those in Prince George's County. At Marion Center Area Secondary School in Pennsylvania, IDs are only used for purchase of free and reduced-cost lunches. There is no requirement that students carry IDs with them.

At Spring High School, near Houston, Texas, IDs are a part of the regulated campus. "We want students to carry IDs every minute of every day," notes Principal Gene LaForge. He was able to keep costs down by striking an agreement with a local photography studio. They take the pictures in exchange for the opportunity to take class pictures each spring. Currently, the cards are not bar-coded, but he hopes to expand the system over time.

Confronting a Trespasser

And what should you say to a trespasser in your halls? Here is a suggestion from Peter Blauvelt, president of the National Alliance for Safe Schools.

Walk up to that person, and in your most forceful, yet non-threatening, voice, announce "Oh, there you are." This makes it clear to the visitor that you know what is going on in your school, who belongs there and who does not — and that you will track down those who walk through the school without permission.

Continue walking to the school office with the visitor while stating "You must have missed the sign requiring all visitors to register. Let's go to the office now, so you can do that — and we can cancel that call to the police."

—Una Hildebrandt

Successful Use of Closed-Circuit Television (CCTV)

If you are considering CCTV, learn from the experience of others:

Remember that technology is not a substitute for human beings. CCTV may be a valuable tool, but safety still depends on adults interacting with and keeping an eye on students.

Hire an independent expert to help you assess your school's needs and the cost of installing the needed equipment, even if you have received a grant to do so. An independent assessment will help ensure that you do not pay more than you need to.

Make sure a decision to install CCTV is justified by need and that key constituencies support it.

Visit other schools that have installed video equipment. Interview administrators about their experience, why they placed cameras where they did, and the impact cameras have had on vandalism, fighting, and crime. Ask about other schools' experience with vendors and prices.

Look closely at several vendors. In addition to cost, ask about training, service, and responsiveness in the event of problems.

Weigh the trade-offs between color and black and white. Black and white is cheaper than color, and some experts find that black and white offers better resolution and clarity. A still picture taken from a tape is reported to be clearer than one made from a color tape.

Be consistent from building to building in the equipment you choose. If administrators move to a new building, they should still be familiar with the CCTV equipment.

Keep the wiring away from high voltage equipment. Such equipment can distort the picture received from the camera.

Keep cameras out of bathrooms, locker rooms, and class-rooms. The right to privacy, and the legitimate objection of teachers make these areas off-limits.

Follow up on all emergency alarms, calls to 911, etc. Students may be testing the system, and they must know that such behavior will be punished.

Do Metal Detectors Really Keep Schools Safe?

We heard it after the tragic killings at a Pearl, Miss., school. And we heard it again after more shootings at a Peducah, Ky., school: "Install metal detectors in the schools to keep guns out!"

Indeed, many school districts have brought metal detection equipment into schools in an attempt to protect students and employees from gun violence. But just how effective are metal detectors in making schools safe? Are they really worth the enormous cost in purchase price, staff training, and maintenance?

Some who work in school security believe metal detectors are an important element in ensuring a safe school environment, while others believe they are not effective at all.

The Benefits of Metal Detectors

"Metal detectors are helpful in schools where there is a high incidence of weapons brought into the building," says Samuel Martin, president of Martin Security Resources, Inc., of Duncanville, Texas. His firm provides security management consulting services to schools and other institutions.

Steve Hollingsworth, a police lieutenant with Portland (Ore.) Public Schools, says his district uses metal detectors on an as-needed basis in middle schools and high schools because they keep schools safe and secure. "We have seen a decline in the number of weapons being brought into Portland schools," he says.

Random use is the reason. Because the devices are sometimes in use and sometimes not, and some days at one school and some days at another, Hollingsworth believes students know there is always the possibility of detection if they try to sneak a weapon into school. Consequently, students stop trying.

One of the most effective uses of metal detectors, according to Peter Blauvelt, director of the National Alliance for Safe Schools, in College Park, Md., is to provide protection during activities taking place in a confined space.

"For school dances, plays, athletic events, and other events held in a gymnasium or auditorium," says Blauvelt, "a walk-through metal detector or a hand-held 'wand' could be effective in keeping weapons out."

Generally, Blauvelt believes hand-held metal detectors are more effective than the walk-through type. Rather than requiring all students to file through a walk-through machine, the wand can be used on any student suspected of carrying a weapon.

"The wand is not intrusive," he says. "I can quickly and easily find out whether a student sets off the equipment and then pursue it from there."

Kenneth Trump agrees that hand-held wands can be more effective than stationary walk-through models. "When used on a random basis," says Trump, director of the Cleveland (Ohio)-based National School Safety and Security Services, "the hand-held wand takes little time and is not intrusive. And it keeps students aware that a weapon could be detected at any time."

Problems with Metal Detectors

Many in the school security field, even some who believe there is a place for metal detectors in schools, are concerned about a variety of problems associated with such equipment. "Metal detectors give schools a false sense of security," says Alex Rascon, retired chief of the San Diego (Calif.) City Schools Police Force. He points out that many students have outsmarted the equipment.

This concern is legitimate, says Martin. "There are videotaped instances where students have passed through metal detectors and gone

Tips for Using Detectors Effectively

Whether and how to use metal detection equipment are important decisions. The following points may help you decide what is best for your particular school or school system:

- Remember that each school's security needs are unique. The decision to install metal detectors should depend on: whether the school has a weapons problem; other safety resources available; the cost of metal detection equipment; available staff; funds for adequate training; and school design.
- Do not view metal detectors as a panacea, but as one possible element in a much broader school security program.
- Be "consistently inconsistent" in the use of metal detectors. In other words, make sure students cannot predict when and where the device will be used.
- Learn about the many tricks that can be used to circumvent metal detection equipment.
- Periodically re-evaluate the school's security needs. As the situation changes over time, decisions about whether and how to use metal detectors may need to change as well.
- If metal detectors are to be used, be sure that clear policies and procedures are developed for their use. Such documents should be approved by administrative personnel and legal counsel.
- Consider training parent volunteers to operate metal detectors as a way to save money, while also involving the community in school safety.

to isolated windows in the school where friends have passed weapons to them." Or, students may hide guns somewhere outside the building and then get them when they're outside for gym class or other reasons.

The physical structure of many schools also makes the use of metal detectors ineffective, says Rascon. In California, for example, many schools have multiple buildings, many entrances, lots of windows, and open grounds. He maintains that in such schools a metal detector at a single entrance is not a deterrent.

Perhaps the biggest downfall — both real and perceived — of metal detectors is cost.

A walk-through metal detector costs about $2,000–$4,000, says Martin. Hand-held wands are less expensive, but both types incur similar costs for staff and training in the equipment's proper use. In addition, explains Martin, staffers must also learn how to calibrate the equipment. "The machine must not be so sensitive that it is set off by a zipper, but it must be sensitive enough to detect a knife," he says.

Walk-through metal detectors can be time-consuming. Under ideal conditions, Blauvelt says, 400 students per hour can be screened with a walk-through machine, "but it never works that way." Kids bunch up, some set off the machine with their jewelry, and others refuse to walk through the machine at all.

In certain schools, the presence of metal detectors can detract from the atmosphere in important ways, says Martha Henninger, a school psychologist in a large alternative school in West Sacramento, Calif. "We emphasize a counseling and therapeutic approach here," she says. "Metal detectors would change that nurturing environment."

Henninger's school has adopted other safety measures, including a full-time police presence.

—April Moore

Integrating Crime Prevention Resource Officers

Communication, Defined Responsibilities Make Programs Work

Clearly defined roles and responsibilities can forecast success for school resource officers in schools, according to two principals who manage resource officer programs.

While job descriptions vary, resource officers' roles and responsibilities in the school are clear: be a visible and positive presence for students and staff, conduct preventive programs, and work with school administrators and local law enforcement to maintain a safe environment in the school.

It is critical to the success of the program that the officer and staff feel that he or she is a resource for both staff and students to improve safety, says Carole R. Shetler, principal of Atlantic Community High School in Delray Beach, Fla. To enhance the officer's job performance, school administrators need to include them in the decision-making process.

"A good example is a recent staff meeting held to debrief administrators following the first football game of the season," she says. "We wanted to review how traffic, security and parking went for the game. The people who came to the meeting included the athletic director, the assistant principals in charge of facilities and disciplines, and the resource officer who oversaw security." The school resource officer is a key person with additional knowledge about the issues who should be included in meetings such as this, says Shetler.

Many resource officers go into classrooms to lecture on preventive programs, become involved in extracurricular clubs, and are visible and accessible in the schools during times when students are present. In addition, officers are featured on the school's closed circuit television several times a year, further expanding their visibility with students.

Role in Deterring Crime

Investigating and deterring criminal conduct is a primary reason the resource officer is in the school. He or she functions as an adviser to administrators, a law enforcement officer, and a mentor to students and faculty who provide tips to resolve problems or make arrests.

Determining who is responsible for checking illegal behavior is the role administrators and resource officers find most difficult to define.

"I have a lot more rights than a policeman does to conduct searches," says Daniel Parrett, principal at Venice, FL, High School. The school handbook states that administrators may conduct locker searches. The resource officer, however, needs probable cause to conduct a search.

Before beginning a search, however, he consults with the school resource officer, then turns over evidence to the officer, who pursues the appropriate legal action. Even with clearly defined responsibilities for her resource officers, Shetler says school administrators must be consulted when a student is arrested because the illegal activity may also violate school policy and require disciplinary measures.

"Working collaboratively is one of the keys to developing a program that works," she says. "None of us on staff would think of interfering in an arrest situation, but we will assist the resource officers and gather information to see if the conduct code is also in violation."

The ability to develop rapport with students gives many resource officers an edge that permits them to be proactive, rather than reactive, to criminal activity in schools. "School resource officers are the envy of many seasoned detectives, because of their ability to solve crimes through the rapport the officers establish with the youth of that school and the community," says Curt Lavarello, president of the National Association of School Resource Officers and a practitioner at Shetler's school.

A crime was solved quickly because of the rapport Lavarello and Shetler's other resource officer built with faculty and students. Several students glued 150 locks on the school, preventing officials from getting in Monday morning and causing about $8,000 in damage.

"I knew that morning that the problems this caused were too big and dramatic for people involved not to brag about it," says Shetler. A teacher told a resource officer about a conversation she overheard between students that helped break the case within 24 hours.

Training Is Crucial

Most resource officers already have law enforcement experience, but Shetler says they need to learn the school's culture and how they will operate at school. This generally takes place through meetings with key school administrators, where expectations are clearly stated.

"When I begin working with a new officer or with a new program, I want to bring that person on board as part of the school team," she says. "When you have 200 employees, including faculty and other support staff, one or two resource officers can really see themselves as a lone ranger out there. I think it is important that does not happen."

For more information, contact: Carole R. Shetler, principal, Atlantic Community High School, Delray Beach, FL, 561/243-1500; Daniel Parrett, principal, Venice High School, Venice, FL, 941/488-6726; Curt Lavarello, president, National Association of School Resource Officers, e-mail: Resourcer@aol.com, or call NASRO at 561/736-1736.

Security Safeguards
PREVENTION OF VIOLENCE

The Latest in Security Threats: Homemade Bombs

Explosive Situations

New times mean new crimes, and the latest are homemade bombs and anonymous bomb threats, says school safety consultant Kenneth Trump.

"We may be worrying about a school safety issue that has been big for a long time, like gang activity, when, in fact, many of the troublemaking students have moved on to new forms of criminal activity," says Trump.

In this case, widespread Internet access may be partially to blame. Any student with a Web browser can find instructions for making explosives. Says Jim Mesterharm, law enforcement manager with the U.S. Attorney's Office in the Northern District of Indiana, "It's just a matter of time until a bomb planted in a school actually goes off."

Administrators Seek Information

Mesterharm's office and the federal Bureau of Alcohol, Tobacco, and Firearms (BATF) recently sponsored a standing-room only workshop on how to handle bombs and bomb threats. Kevin Kocher, a Marion, Ind., high school principal who attended the workshop, learned that his school wasn't adequately prepared for a bomb situation.

"We thought we had a plan for responding to a bomb threat — evacuate the building," he says. "But there, the plan stopped. We really had no idea what to do next, or what to do if the threat proved to be a real bomb."

Trump says that bomb-related information is badly needed.

He described one incident in which a teacher spotted a student planting a pipe bomb. The teacher picked up the bomb, carried it to the office, and placed it on the principal's desk. The principal then carried the bomb outside to the parking lot. In another example, a school custodian found a lunch box wrapped in tape and wires, with a note saying it was a bomb that would explode. The custodian picked up the box, set it down again, and then opened the building to students.

"A full 18 minutes elapsed from the time he found the suspicious object until the time he called the police," says Trump.

What Should You Do?

Advance planning prepares schools to deal with bombs and bomb threats. Take these steps to plug holes in your response plan:

1. Meet with local law enforcement and BATF officials to develop response procedures.

You may borrow from other schools' contingency plans, says Mesterharm, "but every school needs its own site-specific plan." Stress the importance of immediately contacting law enforcement when a suspicious package is found or a threat received.

2. Identify the administrator(s) who will be in charge when a bomb crisis occurs.

Notify all staff, as well as law enforcement and fire department officials, of their identity.

3. Establish an evacuation plan.

Make sure the site to which students and staff are evacuated is within walking distance — but far enough away to be safe from an explosion.

Students at Kocher's school evacuate to the football stadium. But if police determine that site is unsafe, then, by prior arrangement, school buses transport students and teachers to a nearby college.

Be sure to talk with nearby businesses or facilities about receiving students if it becomes necessary to transport them farther than the usual evacuation site. "Plan for cold weather," says Larry Watkins, staff assistant for school safety with Flint (Mich.) Community Schools. "You can't make everyone wait at an outdoor site."

4. Train staff on responding to potential bombs and evacuation.

Because it frequently is the custodian who discovers a bomb, or the secretary who receives the phoned-in threat, make attendance at the training mandatory for all staff. The sessions should specifically address how to recognize a bomb and how to move students to a safe location.

At Kocher's school, the decision to evacuate is spread by word of mouth. He avoids the public address system because it may set off a device. Instead, he notifies two particular teachers, who notify two additional teachers. The relay continues until all teachers are informed.

As teachers usher students out of classrooms, they scan their rooms, looking for anything out of the ordinary. Unusual objects are reported to a designated administrator, who conveys reports to law enforcement. Teachers also take the class attendance book so students can be accounted for at the evacuation site.

Administrators should be assigned to common areas, such as halls, restrooms, and gyms, to scan for suspicious-looking objects before leaving the building.

5. Secure the site where a suspicious-looking object is found.

"Teachers should be trained in how to secure a site, since most of them have no experience in dealing with bombs," says Trump. Evidence must not be moved or touched.

6. Notify parents of the evacuation site.

Secure the entire school so parents do not enter a potentially dangerous situation in search of their children. Kocher says that only after the building is evacuated and all students accounted for, may students be released to parents. The release point is at the evacuation site, of which parents have been previously notified or reminded through press reports.

7. Designate one individual to answer media inquiries.

Do not allow the media access to the students while they are in the care of school administrators and teachers.

8. Place bomb threat checklists near the telephone.

"This is a tool for whoever answers the phone to use to get as much information as possible," says Watkins. The checklist used in Flint schools includes blanks for caller information such as voice characteristics, manner, background noise, and accent. The form also includes spaces for characteristics about the bomb.

9. Equip office phones with caller identification.

Make sure office staff members know how to use the service.

10. Consider removing pay phones from your school.

"When students have legitimate emergency calls to make, they can make them from the office," says Trump.

Watkins says that in Flint, surveillance cameras aimed at the pay phones in one school enabled officials to nab a student who was phoning in a bomb threat from inside the school.

Deciding When to Evacuate

While every phoned-in bomb threat must be taken seriously, Trump says that most calls yield clues about the threat's severity, or lack of it. He believes that when a caller says simply that there is a bomb in the building, it likely is less serious than when the caller says a bomb in the building is going to explode.

"The more information the caller gives, the more likely the threat is real," he says. "When in doubt, it is better to err on the side of safety, even if evacuating the building means more students may phone in false threats just to disrupt school and avoid attending class."

If a suspicious-looking package or object is actually found, contact the police and leave the building immediately. Resume the school day only when authorities have removed the danger or determined that the object is not dangerous.

—*April Moore*

How to Recognize a Pipe Bomb

What Is a Pipe Bomb?

A pipe bomb is a cylindrical container, usually plastic or metal, that contains explosive materials. The container may contain chemicals, be sealed at both ends, and have a fuse or fuses.

What Are the Dangers Associated With Pipe Bombs?

Improvised explosive devices are very unstable. They are extremely sensitive to shock, friction, impact, and heat, and may detonate without warning. Even the smallest devices can cause serious injury or death.

This crime is most prevalent among young males between the ages of 12 and 18. Generally these teenagers excel in academic activities, like to experiment with chemicals, and/or collect literature on bombs and explosives. They may also frequent the Internet.

How Serious a Crime Is Making a Pipe Bomb?

The possession and manufacture of any improvised explosive device, including pipe bombs, is a felony. This crime is punishable by a 25-year imprisonment and a fine of up to $250,000.

This is a very serious offense. Repercussions may include extensive property damage, serious injury, and death.

Courtesy of Montgomery County Fire and Rescue Services, Fire and Explosive Investigations Section, Rockville, Maryland.

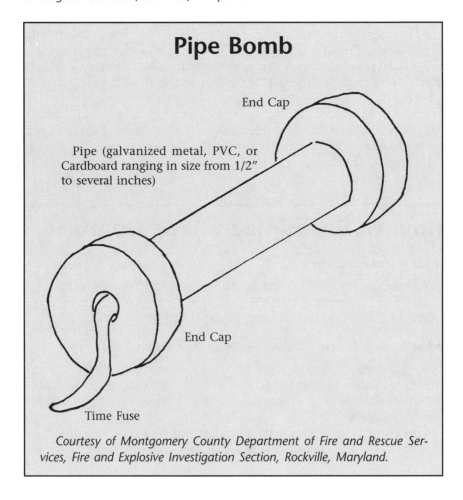

Pipe Bomb

End Cap

Pipe (galvanized metal, PVC, or Cardboard ranging in size from 1/2" to several inches)

End Cap

Time Fuse

Courtesy of Montgomery County Department of Fire and Rescue Services, Fire and Explosive Investigation Section, Rockville, Maryland.

Break the Code of Silence in School: Anonymous Hotlines Offer Promise

It's in every school — the unwritten rule among students that prevents them from relaying safety-related information to an adult. No student wants to be viewed by fellow students as a rat or a snitch. Not only could it mean a diminished reputation or a loss in popularity, but many students also fear that "telling" could result in retaliation — injury or even death.

But when it comes to safety, students are a school's most valuable resource. Much school violence can be prevented if students inform school authorities of other students' weapons and/or plans.

"The majority of kids, under the right circumstances, will let adults know of potential harm or security problems," says Kenneth Trump. "The key is for school officials to create those circumstances."

Ensure Student Anonymity

Students' fears of being discovered are well-founded, says counselor Andi Mallen, of Moorpark (Calif.) High School. "I hear again and again that kids are afraid to tell what they know because the adults don't keep the confidence they promise."

If administrators want students to trust them enough to confide information about weapons, potential violence, and other dangers, administrators have to ensure anonymity. "[For teachers] this doesn't mean reporting the student's tip to the principal and then going to the lounge and telling six other staff members what the kid said," says Trump.

Any commitment to anonymity must come from the top. The principal must stress to administrators, teachers, and other staff members that fulfilling promises of confidentiality is essential in getting students to report what they know.

"Word gets around regarding which adults students feel they can trust," says Mallen.

School-Based Hotlines

One mechanism an increasing number of districts use to encourage anonymous student and community member reports is the 24-hour hotline. There are at least three approaches schools can take to setting up a hotline.

- Districts use their own police department to create and operate a hotline in-house.
- Districts contract the establishment and management of a hotline to a private company.
- The business community takes the initiative. In at least one instance, the business community established and now operates a hotline, saving the school system money and staff time.

School Police-Operated Hotlines

The four-year-old Operation Crime Free Schools (OCFS) in the Clark County, Nev., school district proves that the in-house model works. "Through this hotline, we have received information about weapons, potential suicides, theft, graffiti, and more," says director of police services Jack Lazzarotto. As a result, a number of weapons have been confiscated from students.

The hotline is staffed by school police officers. Upon taking a call, officers refer the information to the appropriate school principal or police officer.

Lazzarotto's department works to publicize the hotline number throughout the district. Posters, in both English and Spanish, decorate school hallways. A local television station airs public service announcements about OCFS. Semi-annual in-services remind teachers of the program.

School-Hired Private Firms

Many districts, especially those without police departments, hire outside firms to run reporting hotlines. Typically, this begins with a district-wide 800-number. Some firms have a live person answering calls, while others rely on tape.

Jim Jones, vice-president of Security Voice, Inc., explains that each caller is assigned a random case number, which the caller and the district use to communicate. Jones' company sends the school a transcript of the message. The school then responds to the caller or requests more information via the caller's case number. Communication between the school and the caller can continue with anonymity as long as necessary through the third-party.

The cost varies. Jones' company charges districts 15 cents per student per month (grades 6-12 or 7-12), or $1.80 per student per year. Florida's Seminole County Public Schools (approximately 60,000 students) pays the Wackenhut Security Corporation $5,000 per year to administer the county's "Save a Friend" hotline, according to district security chief Wolfgang Halbig.

Business-Initiated Hotlines

Greensboro, N.C.'s business community launched — and now operates — Campus Crime Stoppers, an anonymous hotline to which anyone can phone in tips about potentially dangerous school situations. The project is modeled after the widely popular community crime-stopper programs.

In the first month of operation, the hotline resulted in 25 arrests, 11 of which were during the program's first two weeks, according to Don Skinner, chair of the hotline and after-market manager at Copy Pro, a business that sells copying equipment. A volunteer board representing Greensboro businesses schedules volunteers who staff the hotline.

One feature that may contribute to this model's success is the fact that callers can earn rewards for tips — up to $2,500. The amount depends on the tip provided, Skinner says, "and the payments, as well as the calls, are made anonymously."

Rewards come from an annual fundraising telethon that supports both the community hotline and the school hotline. Skinner estimates the telethon brings in about $55,000 per year, "and almost all of that money goes back to the community in the form of rewards in the school and community hotline programs."

Other Anonymous Reporting

A school resource officer (SRO) at one high school created an e-mail hotline by giving his e-mail address to students and the school community. According to Trump, the officer reported significant responses, much better than generally received via traditional hotlines. "This was a creative example of adults adapting to kids' interest in technology," Trump says.

—April Moore

State's School Safety Institute Trains Teachers to Handle Classroom Conflict

While many teachers complain that they are unprepared to deal with aggressive and sometimes violent behavior, Virginia's annual School Safety Institute provides educators there with management skills to confront such problems.

The four-year-old program is a week-long summer course that brings teachers and administrators together with experts who share classroom safety techniques and practical advice for handling difficult classroom situations, says state Department of Education (DOE) school safety specialist Marsha O. Hubbard. The Institute is a collaborative effort between the DOE and James Madison University in Harrisonburg, Va.

"Participants spend a great deal of time working in small groups, discussing what they are learning and sharing their own questions and strategies with each other," says Hubbard.

Anger Management

Anger is a major cause of classroom disruption and aggression, and Institute participants learn effective ways to deal with it.

"I learned that telling an angry student to 'get a grip' is not productive," says Charlottesville elementary school principal, Diane Behrens. "Student anger should not be ignored, but it should be acknowledged and released in a healthy way. It's when anger is expressed in destructive ways that we have trouble in the classroom."

Teachers learn practical ways to help young students release their anger. "By releasing their anger in a physical way, children can move beyond the anger and concentrate on learning," Behrens says.

One technique Behrens brought back to teachers at her school was the "angry bucket." When children are very angry, she says, teachers encourage them to say or write what they are angry about on a block and throw the block into the bucket. "The child then feels he or she has put that anger someplace else and can move on," says Behrens.

Another anger management tool that helps young students release anger is puppets. A teacher who has a ready supply of puppets can encourage an angry child to act out his or her anger.

Teachers of higher grades can help students express anger through writing. Hilda Foster, an Institute participant who teaches third grade in Amelia, says that having an angry student write out his or her anger is helpful. "The student can work through the anger on paper," she says. Foster says this is especially helpful when she is busy with the rest of the class and cannot attend immediately to the angry student.

For students who are so angry that they are out of control, teachers learn techniques for physical restraint without hurting either the students or themselves. Teachers practice the technique and learn how to talk softly and calmingly to the student at the same time.

"Students who are this angry want to calm down, and the restraining technique, combined with calming messages, help them become calm," says Foster. Once students regain self-control, the teacher may want to encourage them to release excess anger through the techniques described above.

Attention and Approval

Institute participants speak enthusiastically about a technique for dealing with students who have behavior problems.

"It's A&A — attention and approval," says Hamilton. "At the start of the day I make a mental note of the most difficult kids and make a point of giving them attention," she says.

Hamilton credits the Institute with making her aware that many students with behavior problems are starved for attention and approval, and behaving disruptively or aggressively is the only way they know to get attention. So Hamilton saves them the trouble. She smiles at these students in the hall, makes friendly comments to them and, in general, gives them the positive attention and approval they need.

Hamilton says that even a small amount of positive attention to an emotionally needy student early in the day can satisfy the craving that might otherwise lead to unsafe, disruptive behavior during the rest of the day.

Safety Bags

Teachers learn from each other at the Institute, and one idea that generated enthusiasm was offered by fourth-grade teacher Anne

Spain. At Spain's Mechanicsville elementary school, each teacher keeps an 'emergency bag' that contains a variety of items that may be needed in case of an emergency.

The bags are bright orange, and each contains:

- the class attendance list;
- a flashlight and extra batteries;
- pens and paper;
- bandages, compresses, and other first-aid supplies;
- medical information about students with special needs;
- a pair of medical gloves;
- emergency telephone numbers;
- tissues; and
- a form to record a missing student.

Keeping Students Focused on Learning

When students are learning, they tend to be too busy to disrupt the classroom. At the Institute, teachers review simple techniques for keeping their students' minds on task:

1. Set high academic expectations. As students work to meet them, they have little time to misbehave. The school day should include little "down time."

2. Move around the classroom. Avoid standing in the same spot in front of the class. Foster says she learned to speak first from one part of the room, then from another. She even sits down sometimes in an unoccupied student seat. "The kids never know where I'm going to show up next, and that helps keep them alert," she says.

3. Keep students on task without embarrassing them. During a lesson, the teacher may ask specific students who appear not to be paying attention what they think about the topic. This approach avoids a confrontation that could embarrass students and result in inappropriate behavior.

4. Model safe, calm behavior. One point stressed to participants is that students model the behavior they see. Teachers have more orderly classrooms when they keep their own voices low. Avoid sarcastic remarks, and treat students with respect.

The orange bag hangs from an adhesive hook in each classroom. Whenever a teacher takes a class outside, the bag comes too. And far from stimulating student's fears about a possible crisis, "the bag is a status symbol," says Spain. "Every child wants to be the one to carry it when the class leaves the building."

Institute participants also hear from a school resource officer (SRO) about how SROs can help teachers maintain safe, orderly classrooms. Hamilton believes this is an important lesson for teachers because "many have not thought of SROs as a resource but only as the last resort in a school administration's attempt to maintain safety."

—April Moore

Anti-Violence Program Helps Students Manage Anger

A study of 790 students paired six schools in King County, Wash., in which students at one school received the training and its partner didn't.

Over the school year, the number of hostile incidents increased at the schools that didn't participate in the anti-violence course, says the report by researchers from the University of Washington in Seattle.

"This is the first time anyone has been able to point out and document behavioral change," based on the curriculum, said Joan Cole Duffell, director of community education for the nonprofit Committee for Children in Seattle, which developed the curriculum.

Students took the 30-lesson course for about 35 minutes up to twice a week. Using picture cards, the Second Step curriculum teaches elementary students how to consider others' feelings, control their impulses, solve problems, and deal with anger.

For instance, when students learn empathy, they learn to notice facial expressions to determine how the other child might feel, and be considerate of those feelings.

They also learn that people may perform the same activities, such as climbing a tree, but may have different feelings about it: One child may enjoy it while another child is afraid.

Each lesson involves the teacher demonstrating a skill, class discussion, and role-playing by students.

Although the behavior changes in the study are considered moderate by the study's researchers, the curriculum can help substantially reduce aggressive behavior teachers must deal with daily, say researchers at the National Center for Disease Control's injury prevention unit, which funded the study.

Accounting for 22 students per classroom and six school hours a day, the changes "amount to about 30 fewer acts of 'negative physical behavior' and more than 800 more acts of 'neutral/pro-social behavior' per class every day," say a group of doctors from the center, which commented on the study in the same journal.

Signing Up

While the university researchers studied two grades that took the curriculum for only 12 weeks, Second Step is designed as a whole-school program with grade-specific curricula from preschool through ninth grade, and includes a parental involvement component that wasn't part of the study.

If schools or districts are interested in starting the program, the Committee for Children will lend copies of the curriculum so teachers and administrators can review it and decide whether to buy it.

If schools sign on, the curriculum costs $250 to $290 per class, depending on the grade level and the number of videos. A three-day teacher training session costs about $300 per teacher.

The curriculum is now used in about 10,000 schools across the United States and Canada.

Single copies of "Effectiveness of a Violence Prevention Curriculum Among Children in Elementary School," are available from Dr. David Grossman, Harborview Injury Prevention and Research Center, 325 Ninth Ave., Box 359960, Seattle, WA 98104, 206/521-1520.

For more information about Second Step, contact Committee for Children, 2203 Airport Way South, Suite 500, Seattle, WA 98134-2027, 800/634-4449.

Student Behavior: The Warning Signs
RED FLAGS

When Students Make Threats . . . Be Prepared

Principals and teachers in Lawrence Township, Ind., ask fewer questions about what to do when students threaten to commit violent acts or talk about violence, thanks to a recently developed response checklist.

The district developed the procedures specifically to address instances when a student threatens to kill others or when a student talks about violent acts, says assistant superintendent for educational support services Duane Hodgin. The checklist has generated wide interest. "School administrators and district officials around the state were interested in using what we came up with," he says.

A few of the suggested responses are described below:

- Document the student's comments; ask the witness(es) — adult(s) and/or student(s) — to record the statements with signature(s) and date.
- Review the student's disciplinary file to look for other incidents of threat, hostility, or aggression.
- Review all of the student's educational records and files to determine whether there are psychological evaluations, educational assessments, or other information relevant to the alleged conduct.
- Invite the student to tell his or her side of the story. Listen carefully, and pay attention to the student's behavior/affect as he or she is telling the story. Take notes on the conversation.
- Check the student, his or her book bag, and locker for possible weapons. Look through the student's notebooks and books for drawings and notes that might bear on the student's propensity to engage in violent or dangerous acts.
- Talk to the student's friends, if they are known, and to his or her teachers. Ask them if they have heard the student make threats or talk about violent acts.
- If appropriate, ask the student if there are guns at home. If so, ask whether he or she has access to them.
- Call the parents/guardian of the threatened student(s) and in-

form them of the incident and the action that has been taken. If charges have been filed, explain to the parents that they have the right to discuss the charges with local law enforcement.

- Following due process procedures, suspend the student from school, depending on the circumstances shown in your investigation.
- Remember that when a student says, "I'm going to kick your ass," the situation is probably quite different from one in which a student says, "I want to/am going to hurt, kill (specific name or a general name)." In the latter situation the student usually provides some detail. Take notes.

—April Moore

Student Hit Lists: Handle with Extreme Care

If one good result has come from the recent tragedies, it is that school officials seem to be taking threats of violence more seriously," says Ken Trump.

More schools are reporting threats to law enforcement — including several recent discoveries of student "hit lists." "Acting decisively to deal with a hit list can only help avoid the experience of looking back after a tragedy and recalling that the student perpetrator had, in fact, told others he was planning to kill, but nobody paid attention," Trump says.

Taking hit lists seriously also gives students the message that making one as a prank or to get attention is unacceptable. Adds Trump, "Just like people know they cannot joke about having a bomb in their bag when they walk through an airport metal detector, students must learn that hit lists will be taken seriously by school officials."

Preventive Action in Tennessee

How should hit lists be dealt with? Following the Jonesboro tragedy, the Williamson County (Tenn.) School District had to deal with two hit lists, both made by elementary school boys. School officials found the lists just a few weeks apart.

The first list named 10 elementary students and was found in the possession of a fourth-grader, in this article called "Boy A." "He admitted having made the list," says Williamson County director of elementary schools Beth Wright. "But while he called it a hit list, he denied having plans to harm any of the classmates listed."

During investigations, Boy A said the appearance of a name on his list meant that the student had guessed a magic word. But other students recalled Boy A stating that he was "going to get a gun and kill" the students on the list. Two students reported that Boy A asked them if they could get a gun for him from their fathers, known by Boy A to be hunters. Boy A told school officials he intended his statements as jokes and he thought others would know he was joking because he laughed after making his comments.

The investigation process included interviews with every teacher Boy A had since kindergarten. No teacher reported behavior problems. Boy A and his parents met with his teacher, the school counselor, and Wright. The parents of all 10 students on the hit list were contacted on the day the list was discovered.

"I suspended [Boy A] for five days, in spite of calls by some parents to expel the student and calls by others to stop making such a big deal over nothing," says Wright. Some parents called for a schoolwide meeting to discuss the situation. But Wright did not hold such a meeting because she thought it may foster panic. For three weeks following the suspension, school officials made frequent searches of Boy A's backpack and desk for weapons. No weapons were found.

Non-disciplinary Intervention

Suspension was only part of the school's response. "We needed to allow the boy the opportunity to succeed without putting others at risk," says Wright. "We wanted him to learn more appropriate behaviors than the one he chose, and to help him address whatever issues led him to take such destructive action."

The school requested, and Boy A's parents agreed to, a psychological evaluation of the boy, with recommendations to be made to the school. Using the professional's guidance, Wright worked with Boy A, his family, and the school to develop a remediation plan.

"We set up an in-school counseling program to help him learn appropriate ways to develop friendships and to deal with conflict," she says. Since he spends a good deal of time at home alone because both his parents work, the remediation plan also addressed constructive ways for him to use his unsupervised time. It also spelled out, in language Boy A could understand, roles for the him, his parents, and school staff. All parties signed the plan following an oral reading. The plan extended through the summer months.

Second Hit List Found

Just weeks after Boy A's hit list was found, another hit list turned up. This time the author was a fifth-grader, called "Boy B." There were four names on his list, titled "People to Kill."

In this case, a classmate saw the list and reported it. "We were better prepared the second time, having gone through it so recently," says Wright. "This time we contacted the parents of the four students named and invited them to the school for a meeting."

Wright asked Boy B's parents if they would like to meet with the parents of the four named students, and vice versa. All were receptive. The school principal facilitated the meeting.

Wright went through a similar process with the students. "The students on the list knew they were part of the problem," she says. "They had teased him terribly, and they regretted it. They even asked if they could each take a day of Boy B's five-day suspension."

Although Wright did not allow the other students to share in Boy B's suspension, she is pleased that they understood their part in the incident and that they wanted to improve their behavior. As with Boy A, a remediation plan was developed, tailored to Boy B's needs.

—April Moore

White House Releases "Early Warning, Timely Response" Guide

If you don't already have a copy of the White House's report released at the beginning of the school year, "Early Warning, Timely Response: A Guide to Safe Schools," you can find it on the Internet at **http://www.ed.gov/offices/OSERS/OSEP/earlywrn.html**, or by calling 1-877-4ED-PUBS.

"Every parent and teacher should be aware of the warning signs exhibited by a troubled child," said Attorney General Janet Reno. "This guide can help save lives and prevent tragedies."

Educators need to know the signs so they can intervene and help such children, while creating a larger network of parents, school officials and students to establish a more nurturing school climate, the guide says.

Extra security and counseling are only part of the solution, the guide says. Schools least prone to violence, the guide says, are those that have high standards of achievement and discipline; have before- and after-school activities; involve families and communities; and work to promote positive relationships among students and staff.

The report presents brief summaries of violence prevention research and crisis response strategies. It identifies these signs as possible predictors of violent behavior:
- social withdrawal;
- excessive feelings of isolation and being alone;
- excessive feelings of rejection;
- having been a victim of violence;
- feelings of being picked on and persecuted;
- low school interest and poor academic performance;
- expression of violence in writings and drawings;
- uncontrolled anger;

State of Our Nation's Youth 1998-1999

	Total	Males	Females
Student Environment	1,041	520	521
Always feel safe in their school	43.9%	42.9%	44.9%
Believe teachers and administrators have taken all necessary steps to make them feel safe and secure	43.2%	40.7%	45.7%
Feel that the behavior of other students in their school interferes with their performance	40.4%	40.2%	40.7%

Source: "State of Our Nation's Youth." Horatio Alger Association of Distinguished Americans, Inc., 1998. Complete study is available on the Internet at http://www.horatioalger.com.

- patterns of impulsive and chronic hitting, intimidating, and bullying behaviors;
- history of discipline problems;
- history of violent and aggressive behavior;
- intolerance for differences and holding prejudicial attitudes;
- drug and alcohol use;
- affiliation with gangs;
- inappropriate access to possession of and use of firearms; and
- making serious threats of violence.

The report also includes a crisis procedure checklist, an action planning checklist for prevention/intervention/crisis response, a list of action steps for students, and tips for parents.

*The White House report, "Early Warning, Timely Response: A Guide to Safe Schools, is available on the Internet at **http://www.ed.gov/offices/OSERS/ OSEP/earlywrn.html** or by calling 800/877-8339.*

—*April Moore*

Student Behavior: The Warning Signs
CULTS AND GANGS

Responding to Cult Involvement

The rapid growth in cult involvement worries many people. Law enforcement agencies, clergy, educators, and animal-rights activists deal with the problem daily.

Ceremonial cult meetings involve activities ranging from animal or human sacrifice, similar to that of Satanism, to sexual orgies — and schools are not immune from these ceremonies. Restrooms, locker rooms, and areas beneath bleachers are often chosen for these or other forms of ceremonies.

It would behoove administrators to search their campuses for strange markings, especially in the above locations. Any suspicion of cult activity should be reported to the police.

Listed below are early warning signs of student involvement in a dangerous cult:

- They isolate themselves from everyone or everything outside of the group.
- There is an "Us" and "Them" mentality. Anyone not belonging to their group is not equal, and is considered evil or of the devil.

- Students will excessively fast, pray, or seem to be under extreme stress, which may result in eating disorders.
- Students will report hallucinations and receiving messages from God through visions.
- There is a fixation on the group and compulsive talking. They often repeat scriptures that the cult emphasizes, which may be taken out of context.
- These students refuse to engage in a conversation about meeting times, the group leaders, or the doctrine. This may be considered to be against their religion and Satanic to talk about the leaders to outsiders.
- Little time is left for family, old friends, and/or other interests with a total devotion to the new group. There is a sense of brainwashing and a wanting to leave the home environment for a new one where they can all be together.
- Those in cults often use confrontational manners in expressing their beliefs.

Statistical Impact of Gangs

Bureau of Federal Prisons representative Robert Harris offers the following statistics about the ways street gangs affect schools and the community:

- The favorite recruiting ground for gangs is middle schools; jail is the second most productive location.
- The annual cost of having metal detectors in a school, including regular maintenance and staff trained to use this equipment, is approximately the same as one teaching position.
- The United States Chamber of Commerce estimates that when gangs move into a retail area, businesses there can expect to lose 25 percent of gross revenue each year.
- The Los Angeles Unified School District currently budgets about $3 million each year solely for graffiti removal.
- According to current projections, homicide will be the leading cause of death in juveniles by the year 2003; homicide now is the leading cause of death among juvenile African-American males.
- A recent National Institute of Justice survey found that 25 percent of students carried a handgun to school in the month before the survey was conducted.

Now that you know the warning signs, the question remains: What can we do?

This is the most important question that family members ask school administrators. Our role is only to help the family by directing them to the appropriate authorities. It is not our role to intervene.

While help is sought, it is important that we not turn students further away and worsen a situation. Therefore, it benefits all involved to follow these few simple guidelines:

- Do not call the group a cult. This only increases hostility and confrontational measures. It may also encourage students to seek the security of the cult and, therefore, leave home.
- Begin to gather as much information about the cult as possible. Contact a local clergyman for reference numbers and help lines.
- Build a relationship between you and the member. All dialogue must be sincere, nonthreatening, and supportive, indicating that you are willing to listen and help.
- Do not send or give money to the "cause" as an act of faith on your part to help. This is a tactic used to support the groups.
- Keep documentation you receive from the group or individual. Sometimes there are encoded messages in them that only experts can understand.

—Melissa Caudle, MEd, PhD

Expert Offers Advice on Slowing Gang Growth

School and Community Involvement Key to Intervention

School district and community cooperation is essential if schools hope to stem gang-related activity and violence, says Robert Harris of the Bureau of Federal Prisons.

Harris, who spoke about youth violence at the National Association of School Safety and Law Enforcement Officers (NASSLEO) annual conference in Branson, Mo., suggests that schools position themselves as facilitators for gang prevention and community education programs, and establish close ties with law enforcement and social service agencies. Schools should not assume they can tackle a gang problem on their own.

"The problem is more complex than individual agencies are equipped to deal with," he says.

Reducing Gang Influence

Steps that you as a school administrator can take to reduce gang impact include:

1. Review missions and activities of school organizations. Some gangs are attempting to legitimize themselves and build political influence by starting community betterment clubs and school social organizations. However, these clubs are often also vehicles for gang recruitment and activity.

Harris recommends that school officials annually review the missions, meeting minutes, and activities of all extracurricular groups to make sure their activities are consistent with their stated purpose.

2. Adopt a weapons policy. If your school doesn't already have a weapons policy, it needs one, says Harris.

When developing a policy, Harris says two elements must be present. First, don't lock yourself into a definition of weapons as just guns or knives. A weapon, says Harris, is "anything used to hurt someone else."

Second, apply uniform and equal enforcement. Without this element, the policy will lose the respect of everyone it attempts to protect — students, parents, and the community.

3. Focus on prevention programs at the elementary and middle school levels. Statistics show that 85 percent of gang members are "associate members" — individuals who associate with a gang for a period of time and then move on to other interests, says Harris.

Associate members' ages typically begin in the 10- to 14-year-old range, with "peripheral" membership beginning as early as age five. Prevention programs that combine counseling with alternative activities to running with a gang work well with these age groups, says Harris. "By the time kids are into high school, their situation with a gang is pretty well settled," he says.

4. Remove graffiti immediately. Harris says this is the "single most effective policy to adopt" in the war on gangs. Graffiti is a gang's sign of ownership and its newspaper. If businesses and schools immediately cover it up, it sends a message to the gang that it's activities won't be tolerated.

Gangs interpret graffiti that is left alone to mean that the property owner feels powerless to stop them.

School officials should photograph all graffiti before covering it, adds Harris. This information is valuable to law enforcement agencies tracking gang activities.

Part II

Crisis Management

CRISIS PROCEDURES

Disciplinary Action or Criminal Investigation? When to Call the Police

For many reasons — but especially the legal ones — it is now more critical than ever that school officials know how to handle the minutes and hours immediately following a safety-related incident, says school police department director Jack Lazzarotto.

"Today's administrators probably have it tougher than anyone," says Lazzarotto, director of the Clark County School District Police Department in Las Vegas, Nev. "In the past, administrators dealt with discipline and that was it. But now [students have] legal representation, and administrators are being put under a microscope."

Attorneys look for missteps in follow-up and investigation — such as principals violating student rights, acting as police officers when they should not, or not involving police when they should.

Police Action vs. Administrative Investigation

A critical distinction made following an incident is whether the situation is criminal or disciplinary in nature. Both incident-types warrant administrative investigation by the principal, but criminal offenses also demand police involvement.

Specifically at issue are witness statements and crime scene protocol. Mistakes in handling these often jeopardize legal cases against accused parties, simply because school administrators don't respond appropriately, or because they fail to respond at all. This, says Lazzarotto, has been "one of the biggest issues" since his department's beginning.

As examples, he describes a principal who ordered custodians to clean up a homicide scene on school grounds. Rather than call the police and have the area taped off, blood and other evidence was removed before the media arrived. In the second example, a principal confiscated a gun and placed it in a school safe until the end of the year — the time when he turned all confiscated items over to district police. After running the gun's serial number, however, police discovered that it was being sought in connection with unrelated crimes.

The principal who confiscated the gun thought he was helping a generally good student out, says Lazzarotto. "But someone's good intent to work with a student doesn't always work out in everyone's best interest."

Know Your Administrative Limits

When something that looks like a crime occurs, or when physical evidence — such as a weapon or illegal substance — exists, administrators must report it, he says. "There is evidence there that law enforcement needs. If someone blows up a toilet in the john, call the police to come in and see if they can identify the explosive. Don't just have custodians clean up the mess."

Lazzarotto's guidelines for determining what is and isn't a crime are simple. He tells principals that if it looks like a crime, report it. If they're not sure, call the police and ask.

"It's not rocket science," he says. "It's like witnessing a crime in a social setting. If you see someone breaking into a house, you call the police and have them deal with it. You don't intervene on your own. The same should be true in schools."

Witness Statements vs. Voluntary Statements

Administrators also must be careful in gathering statements from students who were involved in or who witnessed an incident. Principals don't have authority to mirandize students and shouldn't lead students to believe that they do, nor should they question students in relation to legal statutes.

Administrative questioning and police questioning are different, says Lazzarotto. Police questioning involves due process rights, whereas administrators have more leeway because they are not bound by qualifications such as the "right to remain silent" or the "right to an attorney." Administrators can ask students anything. Students may not answer the questions, but they can be asked.

An administrative investigation and a criminal investigation of the same incident often occur simultaneously. And, while it is important that schools report criminal acts and turn over evidence, it is equally important to remember that these investigations must also be documented separately. Clark County schools use two forms to gather witness statements.

The Voluntary Statement is used by school district police and includes statements notifying students of their rights. The Witness Statement, used by school administrators, asks only for students to state their version of what happened.

An incident that is purely disciplinary and related to school policy, says Lazzarotto, requires only the Witness Statement. Incidents that involve a criminal elements should also be investigated by police, who complete the Voluntary Statement. At subsequent disciplinary hearings, the two documents will support each other and also show that all parties executed their responsibilities according to applicable laws.

Relationships Build Awareness

Knowing "when to do what" is not something that principals learn overnight, especially those who are just beginning to use police resources. The easiest way to learn, though, is by talking.

"If there's not a police agency in the district, then develop a rapport with the agency of jurisdiction," says Lazzarotto. "Have law enforcement be part of school inservice. One of the things I did, too, as a dean of students, was to attend police inservices and learn about what they do. That was very helpful to me. There's nothing inherently wrong, as a principal, to not know about law enforcement. The wrong thing is to do nothing about it."

Taking Witness Statements

■ Use the Witness Statement as a cooling off period. When students were sent to his office, Lazzarotto immediately put them to work filling out their own statements. This gave students a chance to say in their own words what happened, to think about what happened, and to come down to a less emotional level. He also used that time to send notices to the students' teachers asking them for their input on the students' recent behavior and academic progress.

■ Keep an open ear for criminal activity. What begins as a non-criminal incident may turn out to involve weapons or drugs and must be reported to police. When students mention these things in Witness Statements, principals should make special note of it. They can finish the interview as necessary, but the criminal information must be turned over to police so that angle can be investigated as well.

■ Don't press students on legal issues. If questioning a student about a gun, for example, don't force him or her to answer. The last thing you want, says Lazzarotto, is for a student to say later in a police report that the principal "made me say this." If a criminal issue is clearly at hand and students refuse to cooperate, use routine disciplinary measures that any student refusing to cooperate would suffer, and turn the specific legal matter over to police.

—April Moore

Principals' Emergency Checklist

1. Conduct an immediate assessment.

a. Confirm and ascertain the type of incident.
b. Obtain essential information (what happened, who was involved, what did witnesses see, how the incident was started, etc.).

2. Summon help.

a. Call 911. Have someone stay on the line with 911 operator.
b. Have someone else notify school district emergency notification point and Public Information Officer.
c. Implement site and district crisis management plans.
d. Gather school staff assigned to emergency duties.
e. Direct nonessential staff to a safe area.

3. Sound warning to school staff.

a. Use emergency warning and condition signals (entire site).
b. Employ immediate sheltering actions for those exposed to danger.
c. Ensure that all others are sheltered in place or moved to a safer location if possible.
d. Signal instructions.

4. Lock down building, secure areas, monitor situation.

a. Lock exterior doors.
b. Lock interior doors where possible.
c. Assign staff to secure specified and prearranged areas; monitor conditions.
d. Recognize need and be ready for contingencies.

5. Wait for police.

a. Keep responding units updated on situation via 911.
b. Assemble witnesses and victims.
c. Suggest possible areas for staging, command post, emergency medical services, etc.
d. Gather key information for law enforcement.
e. Maintain event and status log.

6. Stabilize elements of situation if safe to do so.

a. Care for injured (ensuring safety for those assisting).
b. Give ancillary staff instructions.
c. Protect crime scene, evidence.

7. Work with police to resolve situation.

a. Stay at command post, supporting incident commander.
b. Provide information, including incident-specific knowledge, site background and resources, and special staff resources, abilities, training, etc.
c. Coordinate school response:
   — onsite
   — off-site (staging areas, hospitals, etc.)
   — district

8. Signal "all clear."

a. See that emergency medical care is provided.
b. Account for all students and staff onsite or at hospital or other off-site locations.
c. Notify parents/guardians.
d. Support law enforcement follow-up activities.
e. Debrief staff.
f. Arrange for site security if necessary.
g. Work with specialists:
   — emergency medical/hospitals
   — district crisis intervention team
   — Public Information Officer
   — facilities cleanup and repair support

9. Initiate recovery and follow-up activities.

    a. Brief staff and provide (access to) support.

    b. Plan for resumption of school ("next day" plan).

    c. Arrange for physical plant cleanup and repair.

    d. Begin long-term recovery planning.

Source: Stephanie Kadel and Joseph Follman, Hot Topics: Usable Research, Reducing School Violence, *SERVE, SouthEastern Regional Vision for Education, Affiliated with the Florida Department of Education and the School of Education, University of North Carolina at Greensboro, SERVE 345 S. Magnolia Drive, Suite D-23, Tallahassee, FL 32301-2950 Phone 800/352-6001; Fax 904/922-2286, March 1993.*

Teachers' Emergency Procedures

1. Immediate recognition and assessment.

    a. Warning signals, codes, information from office or others.

       — **Signal/Condition A**: Staff alert for intruder positions in hall, report sightings.

       —**Signal/Condition B**: Lock doors, secure building, secure rooms, await instructions.

       —**Signal/Condition C**: Take immediate sheltering actions.

       —**Signal/Condition D**: Emergency over, all clear, stay put, await instructions.

    b. Direct observation or knowledge of conditions — look, listen, etc.

    c. Report significant information to office.

    d. Be alert to conditions and threat source.

2. Immediate sheltering actions.

    a. Lock door(s).

       — Do not chain or barricade.

       — Do not lock out those needing shelter.

    b. Shelter in place.

       — Use basic duck and cover techniques: lie flat, face down, on floor; cover head, get under tables/desks if possible.

       —In classrooms, stay away from windows, doors, and outer walls; watch for shattered glass.

—In other areas and on buses, use basic duck and cover techniques.

—In open areas, use objects immediately available in the open (trees, bushes, walls, etc.) for shelter; lie down, stay motionless.

c. Move to shelter in different place if it is safe to do so. If current location is judged too dangerous, move to possible alternate locations in hallway or in other rooms or areas in the building.

d. Evacuate the building (different from fire or bomb threat).
— Use a safe, clear, secure route.
—Identify an assembly point.
— Be ready to seek immediate cover.

3. Other immediate action.

a. Care for injured, but do not expose yourself to danger.

b. Close drapes/curtains/blinds ONLY if safe to do so.

c. Turn out lights if it is safe to do so.

d. Be ready to move instantly (know possible evacuation routes, including windows).

e. Have an accurate account of children (take class record book with you if the class is evacuated).

f. If possible, report status or significant changes to office/incident command post.

4. Actions during resolution of emergency.

a. Care for students.
— Deal with panic/hysteria/stress reactions.
—Provide psychological first aid.
— Provide for needs of handicapped students.

b. Follow instructions of police and principal. (Police are in charge; principal and other staff support their efforts.)
— Be prepared for police to suddenly appear.
— Be ready to move, follow special instructions.

c. If you and your students are taken hostage
— Stay calm.
— Don't be a hero.
—Follow instructions of captor.
— Cooperate, be friendly if possible; don't argue with or antagonize captor or other hostages.
—Inform captors of medical or other needs.
— Be prepared to wait; elapsed time is a good sign.
—Don't try to escape; don't try to resolve situation by force.

— Be observant and remember everything you see or hear.

— If a rescue takes place, lie on the floor and await instructions from rescuers.

d. Be prepared for the unexpected; think of possible courses of action for various contingencies.

5. Actions to take following the "All Clear," signal.

a. Check yourself and your students for injuries.

b. Account for all students. Stay put and wait for instructions.

c. As accurate information becomes available, explain to students what has happened and what will happen
next. Allow them to ask questions, express feelings, etc.

d. Monitor children who were directly involved or direct witnesses and identify them for police investigators.

e. Preserve any physical evidence (don't touch if possible) and notify police about it.

f. Stay with your students until they are reunited with their parents.

— Debrief officials and receive instructions for recovery/follow-up activities.

— Take advantage of personal support services.

— Go off duty — take care of yourself.

Source: Stephanie Kadel and Joseph Follman, Hot Topics: Usable Research, Reducing School Violence, *SERVE, SouthEastern Regional Vision for Education, Affiliated with the Florida Department of Education and the School of Education, University of North Carolina at Greensboro, SERVE 345 S. Magnolia Drive, Suite D-23, Tallahassee, FL 32301-2950 Phone 800/352-6001; Fax 904/922-2286, March 1993.*

Gun Confiscation Checklist

Many educators report ongoing concerns about the procedures to follow if they are confronted by someone with a gun or if they find a gun on campus. Common sense and professional training are the two best resources available to educators, as well as familiarizing yourselves with gun safety procedures before an incident occurs. Here are some recommended steps that should be part of your school's procedure and shared with all faculty and staff members.

1. Assess the situation and determine if it is life-threatening.

Life-threatening situations require an immediate action in order to avoid serious injury or death to someone. At the time of a life-threatening crisis, you cannot wait for law enforcement to arrive and take action. Each school must determine what as classifies life-threatening. If a staff member determines that a crisis is life-threatening, then the administrator involved should take the action necessary to provide for the safety of the staff and students.

2. Notify the principal immediately to activate a Red Alert status.

In a life-threatening crisis, notification of the principal isn't always easy for the staff person involved in the crisis. Staff and faculty should be cross-trained to identify situations and provide notification on behalf of their peers.

3. Isolate the student or intruder suspected of having a gun if possible.

Consider the student or intruder as dangerous. Remain calm. Do not say or do anything that will further aggravate the individual. Remove staff and students from the area if possible, including yourself. This is easier said than done. Common sense prevails in these situations. If you or the entire class is taken hostage, cooperate with the perpetrator. Try to keep students calm and stress the importance to them of following instructions.

4. Avoid exciting the intruder.

Talk in a calm manner with a very soft voice. Try to distract the intruder with casual conversation until the police arrive and establish communication. They are trained to deal with specific hostage situations.

5. Wait for the police.

6. If the situation is not life-threatening, do not try to take the gun from the student or the intruder.

The risk factor increases for accidental death or injury from gunfire in these situations. Leave the confiscation to trained individuals on the crisis response team or law enforcement office.

7. If you find a gun on campus, do not touch it, and do not let the gun out of your sight.

The chances of a gun falling into the wrong hands increases. Notify the nearest crisis team member or principal. Stay by the gun and send another staff member or responsible student to notify the office. Do not be tempted to take the gun to the principal yourself. There are two reasons for this. First, if you don't know how to handle a gun, you could accidentally fire it. Second, you do not want your fingerprints on the gun. It will be easier for authorities to lift prints from the gun for possible identification during the police investigation.

8. If a student or intruder hands you a gun, remain calm.

Consider the gun loaded and do not point it at anyone or anything, do not touch the trigger or other moving parts, and do not attempt to unload the chamber. Hold the gun by the handle and do not put your finger on the trigger. Instead, lay your finger along side the trigger or firmly grasp the entire handle. Point the gun away from people and valuable objects.

9. If at all possible, never touch the gun.

—*Melissa Caudle, MEd, PhD*

How to Respond to a Bomb Threat

School violence is now a familiar part of the daily news and, consequently, there is a chance for copycat acts. Fortunately, the vast majority of bomb threats made to schools are pranks, and no lives are in danger. However, this does not minimize the potential for the real thing. Bomb threats must always be taken seriously.

With a few established procedures, threats can be handled in an efficient and safe manner. The person receiving the call, for example, should immediately document it. If the caller indicates the specific make of the bomb, the location, and the exact time it will explode, chances are good that it's the real thing, and the building should be evacuated. If the caller could not identify these things, proceed with caution and notify the police and fire department. Also at this time, the following steps should be initiated:

1. Announce over the intercom the bomb threat code word.

At no time should the words "bomb threat" be used in the code. An example of a coded statement is, "Attention teachers, Ms. Canary's meeting with the safety committee will be today in the library."

2. Act on the coded warning.

All employees should be trained to recognize the code statement and to act appropriately when they hear it. Teachers should look around their classrooms for unusual objects and to see if items have been moved. Teaching should not be interrupted while they do so. The rationale is that those most familiar with individual rooms are in the best position to recognize changes to the environment or any unusual packages or objects.

All other personnel — janitors, administrators, monitors, etc. — should have assigned areas that they, too, immediately search. When checks are complete, each staff member posts a note outside of his or her door that the check is complete and that nothing unusual was found At this time, the principal evaluates the situation before taking further action. There should be no movement of classes.

3. Evacuate if appropriate.

After evaluating the reports, conduct any necessary evacuations as if they are fire drills, in order to avoid panic.

Schools may enlist additional help in developing bomb threat procedures from local police and fire departments, as well as the local or state Office of Emergency Preparedness. These agencies are quite helpful in assisting schools with bomb threat procedures.

—Melissa Caudle, MEd, PhD

Bomb Threat/Explosion Procedures

In the event that a call or warning is received indicating that a bomb has been placed in a school building or on school grounds, the following procedures are recommended. *NOTICE:* Detailed plans for bomb threat procedures with local authorities should be known only to administrative personnel in the school; therefore, this information plan should be available only to building staff members.

A Suggested Plan of Action

If the superintendent receives a call reporting that a bomb has been placed in a building, he/she will immediately:

a. Call the building principal.
b. Call authorities.
c. Arrange for staff assistance.
d. Call 911. Indicate if this was a *threat, if there is a fire, or if there has been an explosion.*

If a principal receives a call, he/she will immediately:

a. Evacuate *all* students and *all* teachers from the building. (Distance of at least 150 feet or maximum distance, simultaneously, if possible.) Call 911. Indicate if this was a *threat, if there is a fire, or if there has been an explosion.*
b. Call the Superintendent of Schools.

   c. Collect and record the following pertinent data:
     1. What time was the call made?
     2. The date
     3. Who made the call?
     4. Was the location of the bomb given? If so, where?
     5. Any other information from Telephone Procedures "Bomb Threat Checklist" (see below).
   d. If time permits, windows should be opened and any coats grabbed from room (elementary) and lights turned off.
   e. If time permits, initiate search and find procedures.
   f. The completed Bomb Threat Telephone Checklist is to be submitted *within 24 hours* to the Superintendent of Schools.
   g. Teachers and students will *stay in assembly area until authorized by superintendent, principal, and/or ranking member of local authorities* to:
     1. Dismiss school.
     2. Transport students to another school or schools.
     3. Return to building.
   h. *Any decisions concerning the dismissal of school pupils and subsequent action after the above procedures have been followed are the prerogative of the County Superintendent of Schools.*

If teacher, secretary, or any school service personnel receives information of a bomb threat, they will immediately notify the building principal who will then follow through.

Courtesy of T.A. Lowery Elementary School, Shenandoah Junction, West Virginia, Jefferson County Schools, Charlestown, West Virginia, 304/728-7250.

Telephone Procedures Bomb Threat Checklist

This form should be completed by the person who received the bomb threat call, and the information should be made available to the fire marshal and/or police upon their arrival at the school building.

Do not interrupt the caller! Be calm. Be courteous. Notify supervisor by prearranged signal while caller is on the line.

Name of Operator
Time
Date
Caller's Identity: __Adult __Juvenile __Approximate Age
Sex: __Male __Female
Origin of Call:
__Local __Long Distance __Booth __Internal (within building)

Voice Characteristics:
__Loud __High Pitched __Raspy __Intoxicated __Soft __Deep
__Pleasant __Other
Speech:
__Fast __Distinct __Stutter __Slurred __Slow __Distorted
__Nasal __Lisp __Other __
Language:
__Excellent __Good __Fair __Poor __Foul __Other
Accent:
__Local __Foreign __Not Local __Region __Race
Manner:
__Calm __Rational __Coherent __Deliberate __Righteous __
Angry __Irrational __Incoherent __Emotional __Laughter
Background Noises:
__Factory Machines __Bedlam __Music __Office Machines __Trains
__Animals __Quiet __Voices __Party Atmosphere __Mixed
__Airplanes __Street Traffic __Other

Pretend difficulty with hearing. Keep caller talking. If caller seems agreeable to further conversation, ask questions like:
1. When will it go off?
   __Certain hour __Time remaining
2. Where is it located?
Building_____
Area_____
(Did caller appear familiar with building by his description of bomb location? __Yes __No)
3. What does the bomb look like?_____
4. What kind of bomb?_____
5. What will cause it to explode?_____
6. Did you place the bomb? __Yes __No
7. Why did you place the bomb?_____
8. What is your address?_____
What is your name?_____

Action to Take Immediately After Call

Notify your supervisor. Talk to no one other than instructed by your supervisor.

Write Out the Message in Its Entirety.

Courtesy of T.A. Lowery Elementary School, Shenandoah Junction, West Virginia, Jefferson County Schools, Charlestown, West Virginia, 304/728-7250.

Sample Written Notice to Parents Re: Crisis

TO: Parents
FROM: Principal

RE: Unfortunate incident

Today we had (or were made aware of) an unfortunate incident. Although our students and staff handled the situation well, I want to tell you about it so you will know the facts and so you will be better able to talk about it with your child.

[Briefly describe the facts of the situation. It may help to keep to who, what, why, when, where, etc. Include the current status of the situation, e.g., hospitalized, funeral arrangements (or directions to read the newspaper, listen to the radio, watch for additional information that will be sent home with each child, etc.).]

We did have a team of people (counselors) in our school today to help our students. These counselors were available for students to talk with about their concerns regarding the incident.

Your child may express concern to you about what happened. The concern may be shared today, next week, or even later. The best way you can help is to listen and be reassuring. If there is a way we can be of assistance to your child, please call the office.

Thank you for your support at this difficult time.

Courtesy of Jon Mattison, Grover Cleveland Middle School, Zanesville City Schools, Zanesville, Ohio.

Part III

Legal Issues, Policies, and Procedures

Congress Poised to Debate Safe Schools Policy, Funds

The federal government, eager to prevent student violence, already funds anti-drug and school safety programs throughout the nation. But the Clinton administration wants to do even more, while some critics are calling for new approaches, including scrapping the nation's main safe-schools legislation altogether.

Congress last year appropriated $566 million for programs under the 1994 Safe and Drug Free Schools and Communities Act (SDFSCA) to support the use of "comprehensive, integrated approaches to drug and violence prevention," according to the Clinton administration's budget summary.

President Clinton, in his plan for fiscal 2000, asked Congress to modify the SDFSCA program by requiring state education agencies to distribute 30 percent of their formula funds as competitive grants. He wants to fund quality programs in districts with concentrated drug and violence problems.

Get Rid of It

Some education policy analysts, however, say Congress would do better to scrap SDFSCA altogether because its funds are spread too broadly to have a lasting or constructive impact.

Education Secretary Richard Riley recently contributed to the perception of the safe and drug-free schools program's ineffectiveness, telling the House education committee in February that three-fifths of school districts currently receive SDFSCA grants of less than $10,000, or an average grant of $5 per student.

In an April 1999 speech, Riley called for greater community involvement rather than specific legal or congressional action. "More schools and communities need to develop strong peer mediation programs, improve counseling and mentoring efforts, install hotlines, and do whatever it takes to build a supportive school environment for all students," he told the Anti-Defamation League in Washington, D.C.

Andy Rotherham, director of the 21st Century Schools Project at the Progressive Policy Institute, proposed in April that Congress consolidate SDFSCA and other categorical programs authorized under the 1965 Elementary and Secondary Education Act (ESEA). ESEA expires in September, 1999, opening the door for the GOP Congress to reshape it.

"No comprehensive data on the effectiveness of safe and drug-free schools funds exists and meaningful data would be difficult to gather," Rotherham said. "Ample anecdotal evidence suggests that funds are often used ineffectively and that the program lacks a clear focus."

Focus on Drug Abuse

Writing for the Thomas B. Fordham Foundation, author Matthew Rees earlier this year complained that the purpose of the SDFSCA program, discouraging drug abuse, has been broadened to include violence prevention and health education. He said states should be required to evaluate their SDFSCA initiatives more often than once every three years, and he advised the federal government to provide more information to districts about what works in anti-drug education.

"More information must be made available to state and local education agencies about successful curricula, and more efforts must be made to weed out untested programs," wrote Rees, who wants Congress to focus on preventing drug abuse.

The administration last year said it wanted to change the SDFSCA by requiring schools to adopt comprehensive school safety programs. However, the administration has not yet released its bill for rewriting ESEA.

In April, the administration launched its $180 million Safe Schools, Healthy Students Initiative (SSHSI), hoping to create model violence prevention projects in 50 school districts.

SSHSI will be funded in part with $60 million from the Education Department's SDFSCA budget, meaning the program represents $120 million in added money. The government's budget for improving the school environment, then, is $686 million.

Congressional Republicans in April called for a national conference on cultural influences on youth, focusing on the potentially damaging effects of video games, movies, and drug abuse.

"I don't know that there is a consensus out there right now" on the safe and drug-free schools program, said Vic Klatt, education policy coordinator for Republicans on the House Education and the Workforce Committee. "Generally, people look at it as a drug prevention program." Hearings are planned, he said.

California Now Requiring Staff Training in School Safety

Meetings Planned to Inform Universities, School Districts of Resources and Obligations

Educators seeking licensure in California must now show that they have received instruction in school safety principles before they can receive that state's credential.

The requirement makes California the "first and only state to require school safety training in preparation programs for teachers and other educators," according to a report issued by an advisory panel on school violence organized by the Commission on Teacher Credentialing (CTC).

California Senate Bill 2264, which became effective January 1, 1999, requires that teachers, counselors, administrators, and other professionals seeking a credential in pupil personnel services receive training in four areas:

- school management skills that emphasize crisis intervention and conflict resolution;
- developing and maintaining a positive and safe school climate, including methods to prevent the possession of weapons in school;
- developing school safety plans; and
- developing ways to identify and defuse situations that may lead to conflict or violence.

Training curricula are being developed by individual colleges and universities.

The law is related to earlier legislation that directed the CTC to investigate how educators could be better prepared to cope with school violence. An advisory panel of K-12 educators, students, university professors, school board members, community volunteers, credential candidates, law enforcement officers, and people from the private sector studying this issue published its findings and recommendations in October 1995.

Need for Training Is Clear

One problem creating a need for additional staff training, safety officials say, is the disparity between teacher and student backgrounds.

Many teachers and administrators come from white, middle-class homes. As a result, many teachers frequently are unprepared to deal with the ethnic differences among students in urban school districts.

"There's a significant gap between the training that is being provided and the kind of training they need to survive," says Ronald Stephens, executive director of the National School Safety Center in Westlake Village, CA, a national leader in violence prevention training. "A number of teachers who leave the profession following their first experience after college literally are shell-shocked."

Denver Public Schools Director of Safety and Security Ed Ray says the adjustment for teachers and administrators who are unfamiliar with urban schools can be "overwhelming," even for those with experience.

"Suddenly they see gambling in the hallways, students carrying knives, and other typical inner-city problems. For a brand new teacher, it can be a real culture shock. Those who've grown up in the system are better off."

The CTC advisory panel report supports these assertions. Multicultural sensitivity training; conflict management and resolution skills; and interpersonal communication skills were the top three responses from focus groups asked about the type of training most needed to address school violence. Also, survey results showed that nearly 80 percent of teacher-trainers nationwide said their students received no special training related to school violence.

CTC staff consultant Joseph Dear views the new credential requirement as a way to prepare teachers to address a continuum of school violence.

"Teachers and administrators don't need to be trained as police officers," he says. Rather, they need to be trained to better deal with small incidents, such as name-calling, that frequently escalate into serious problems.

Preparatory Programs Include Preventive Elements

No specific guidelines for meeting S.B. 2264's criteria, such as minimum credit hour requirements, have been issued by the CTC. How to best address the topic of school violence is being left to the discretion of individual colleges and universities developing curricula for students who are becoming teachers or administrators.

"Some institutions will have a specific course. Others will integrate the subject into courses they already have. Others will have seminars or workshops or other ways of addressing the requirement to make sure students who are becoming teachers or administrators have that competency," says Dear.

Assistant Professor Ernie Baumgarten of Saint Mary's College of California Graduate School of Education in Moraga says teachers in training there receive violence-related instruction as part of a classroom management course. "One of the early precepts we talk about is that if you don't know what you want [in terms of behavior], then you take what you get," he says.

State Moves to Publicize Report and Law

According to language in the statute, the new safety instruction requirement applies only to individuals now applying for a California credential. It does not apply to professionals who already hold a credential there.

However, Dear expects that many current staff members will learn safety principles through professional growth activities required by the credential renewal process. "[A safety-related curriculum] is one of the avenues they could use to satisfy that requirement," he says.

Currently, the CTC is coordinating regional conferences for K-12 administrators, professional organizations, and college and university officials to discuss implementation of the report's recommendations and the provisions of S.B. 2264. It is also compiling a list of exemplary programs and practices for preventing and coping with school violence to share at the conferences so participants can learn from each other.

For information about training programs offered by the National School Safety Center, call 805/373-9977 or write: National School Safety Center, 4165 Thousand Oaks Blvd., Suite 290, Westlake Village, CA 91362.

"Creating Caring Relationships to Foster Academic Excellence: Recommendation for Reducing Violence in California Schools" was released by the State of California Commission on Teacher Credentialing in October 1995.

FERPA Rules Grant Greater Access To Disciplinary Records

School and college administrators will be freer to share student records under updated Education Department rules.

The changes to the Family Educational Rights and Privacy Act (FERPA), which were enacted in November 1996, permit schools to exchange information regarding disciplinary action for behavior threatening the safety of other students or teachers.

While schools have always been allowed to transfer information when a student changes schools, the new rule expands the roster of situations for which records can be exchanged.

Essentially, a school could release a districtwide notice to inform other schools of a problem student. Schools also may release records to state juvenile justice systems without the student or parents' consent, under the new rules.

FERPA generally bars schools from releasing students' records without their, or their parent's, consent, but Congress made some changes in the 1994 Improving America's Schools Act giving parents more access. Only students age 18 and older can request their records.

The new rules require state education agencies (SEAs), and K-12 and postsecondary schools to give parents, students and juvenile law enforcement agencies freer access to student records.

SEAs must allow parents and students access to an individual student's records kept at the state level. This includes information related to the Individuals with Disabilities Education Act and statewide assessments.

SEAs previously were not required to release this information to parents.

The department also is lifting a requirement that schools maintain a formal student records policy, but schools will have to notify parents and students annually about their rights under FERPA.

"The department does not require schools to individually notify parents or eligible students of their rights, but only that they give notice that is reasonably likely to inform the parents and students of their rights," the rule states.

A Hypothetical Situation: Early Warning Allowed

An Education Department staffer offered a hypothetical situation to explain the rule's boundaries. She said if "school A" is having a football game and a gang of students from "school B" were planning to attend and cause problems, the principal from "school B" could notify officials at the other school that the troublemakers were headed their way.

The department has a sample two-page form available for schools. It provides one model for K-12 institutions and another for postsecondary schools in the Nov. 21 Federal Register.

Institutions would be required to fulfill a request for student records within 45 days, and would be able to charge a "nominal" fee for gathering and copying the documents.

School Law Enforcement Records May Not Be Subject to FERPA Restrictions

Many school officials fear potential liability for disclosing student information to law enforcement or social service agencies, despite knowing that shared information could benefit many at-risk youths.

At the heart of this dilemma lies the Family Educational Rights and Privacy Act (FERPA) — a complex federal law protecting the privacy of students' education records. While the law gives parents the right to review their children's records, schools cannot disclose information to others without parental consent.

What many school officials find confusing, however, is the statute's school law enforcement exemption. Records created by a school law enforcement unit and maintained for law enforcement purposes are not under the purview of FERPA. This information may be disclosed, without prior consent, to anyone, including the media.

To guide schools through the confusion, the U.S. Departments of Justice and Education have jointly issued "Sharing Information: A Guide to the Family Educational Rights and Privacy Act and Participation in Juvenile Justice Programs." The following recommendations come from this publication:

The Limits of the Law

■ Similar information maintained in both education records and law enforcement records is subject to different disclosure terms. Any record of disciplinary action, such as suspension for fighting, is considered an education record. It may not be shared without prior consent. However, school resource officer (SRO) reports of a fight, maintained as part of a law enforcement file, may be shared. School officials also may talk about their experiences with students since personal observations may be disclosed without consent.

■ School districts that do not maintain their own law enforcement units often form partnerships with municipal or county police forces. These arrangements may function according to the above rule as long as the school designates particular police officers as the district's law enforcement unit. To ensure compliance, this designation should be stated in a written contract or memorandum of understanding.

■ FERPA includes an emergency exception, which means that schools are not bound by disclosure restrictions during a safety or health emergency.

■ All school personnel may share information about students that is based on personal observation, provided that information is not based on the contents of an education record (defined to include report cards, health and special education records, surveys and assessments, correspondence with other entities regarding students, and information about parents).

■ Information may be shared with teachers and school or district staff who have a legitimate educational interest. When information is necessary for an educator to fulfill a professional responsibility, that educator may see the information without prior consent.

■ "Directory information" from education records is fair game. This information includes, but is not limited to, the student's name, address and telephone number, date and place of birth, major field of study, dates of enrollment, height and weight for sports, degrees and honors received, educational institution most recently attended, and a photograph. Schools may choose how much directory information to disclose. But they should then give notice of the specific types of directory information they plan to disclose. Parents may retain the right of consent related to directory information.

Information Received by Schools

Although FERPA restricts what information schools can disclose, law enforcement agencies are free to share all information with schools.

If a student commits a crime outside of school, for instance, the police can report the incident to the school. Once received, however, the information becomes part of the education record and is subject to FERPA restrictions.

—April Moore

Schools and school districts risk being taken to court when they don't act on school safety matters. But they also risk lawsuits when they do act, especially when they concern issues of student privacy. The following court cases illustrate the perils of implementing school safety measures, and the need to anticipate troubles that aren't always easy to detect.

JUDICIAL RULINGS

California Court Okays Searches With School Metal Detectors

For the first time in California, a court upheld the legality of schools searching students with metal detectors (February 23, 1998).

The student, a girl in the Los Angeles Unified School District, had been notified before enrolling that the district has a written policy allowing daily random weapons searches with hand-held metal detectors.

School officials are to use "neutral" criteria for conducting searches, according to district policy. In this case, the assistant principal decided to search students who entered the attendance office without hall passes, and those who were up to 30 minutes late for school.

The Tell-Tale Beep

About 10 students were searched. After the metal detector beeped on a girl, Latasha, she was asked to open a pocket, revealing a knife. She was expelled, and was placed on probation in juvenile court.

In her appeal, the student claimed the search was illegal. But the state's court of appeals, in the first ruling on the issue in California, said the search was "minimally intrusive."

"Only a random sample of students was tested," the court said in *People v. Latasha W.* (1998 WL 27958). "Students were not touched during the search, and were required to open pockets or jackets only if they triggered the metal detector."

Although California courts hadn't decided the issue previously, the judges noted that similar searches of students without "individualized suspicion" have been approved by courts in Florida, Pennsylvania, Illinois, and New York since 1992.

A report mandated by California's legislature found that one out of every seven crimes in public schools involves a weapon. The survey also said there were more than 5,400 incidents involving knives in the state's public schools in 1995-96.

But a survey last year by the American Civil Liberties Union of Southern California said that 63 percent of Los Angeles high school students believe metal detectors are not a deterrent to keeping weapons off campus.

Judge Says Anti-Gang Policy Must Be Specific, Up-to-Date

School districts with anti-gang dress codes should keep comprehensive lists of banned apparel, a federal judge ruled in allowing two Texas students to wear rosary beads (September 9, 1997).

The judge struck down the New Caney Independent School District's policy, which defines "gang-related apparel" simply as any attire that is "gang-related."

While the student handbook does define some fashion as gang-related — from baggy pants worn low on the waist to baseball caps — it also states that a specific list of forbidden items is available at the principal's office. But Principal Charles York told the court that no such list exists, except in the head of the school's police officer.

In April 1997, a federal appeals court also voided an Iowa school district's anti-gang dress code because it was too vague to guide the administrators who had to enforce it.

In the Texas decision, U.S. District Judge David Hittner for the Southern District of Texas ordered the administrators to allow high school students to wear rosary beads outside their shirts. The judge said wearing the religious symbols is protected by the First Amendment's guarantee of freedom of expression.

'Homie' Warning

David Chalifoux and Jerry Robertson had been wearing the rosaries at school for several months when the school's gang liaison officer told them that they couldn't keep wearing the beads outside their clothing. The officer said rosaries were identified with a Houston gang called the United Homies.

The officer didn't accuse the students of being gang members; he told them to conceal the rosaries for their own safety.

The principal didn't punish the students, but he told teachers to send the boys to his office if they displayed the rosaries again.

The conservative Rutherford Institute represented the students in their suit, arguing that they have a right to religious expression and that the district's policy is too vague to be enforced.

The school district said it was trying to restrict gang activity, not suppress religious expression, and it needed discretion to maintain order.

School officials testified that compiling a detailed list of gang-related items is impractical because gangs change clothing and symbols often. But the judge said in *Chalifoux v. New Caney* Independent School District (97-1763) it would not be "overly burdensome for the district to provide a definite list of prohibited items and to update that list as needed."

The judge also said that because school officials didn't prove that gangs were a problem, they could not curb the students' "religiously motivated speech."

"This case doesn't mean schools can't regulate gang activity on campus," said attorney Brent Perry, who represented the students. "But they can't shut down religious expression without a very good reason."

Court Says Juvenile Charge Alters Special Ed Placement

Special education law is the most litigated aspect of schooling. When disability issues bump up against school safety concerns, policy-making generally requires a careful understanding of both the Individuals with Disabilities Education Act and the Americans with Disabilities Act.

Before a school files criminal charges against a disabled student, it must notify the parents of the potential "change in placement," a federal appeals court has ruled (January 31, 1997).

The U.S. Sixth Circuit Court of Appeals said a Tennessee school district violated the Individuals with Disabilities in Education Act (IDEA) by charging a hyperactive student with vandalism in juvenile court before consulting his education team.

The three-judge panel unanimously upheld a decision in *Morgan v. Chris L.* (94-6561) by a federal district court.

"It's going to send shock waves," said Perry Zirkel, a professor of education law at Lehigh University in Bethlehem, Pa.

"Some school administrators have been using the notion of trying the juvenile justice system as a 'safety valve' for very bad behavior," he said. "This shuts that door for many of them who already feel hamstrung" under the Individuals with Disabilities Education Act (IDEA).

The National School Boards Association had filed a brief urging the Sixth Circuit to overturn the lower court's decision. "If the school district's action in this case implicates IDEA rights, then the IDEA is also implicated by a call to the police when a student brings an Uzi to school and starts shooting people," it said.

Before Receiving Services

The boy, a middle school student in the Knox County district, was diagnosed with attention deficit disorder. He was taking Ritalin, yet his grades and behavior were worsening steadily.

The school district had not yet reached a decision on whether the boy was considered disabled under IDEA when he vandalized a school bathroom, causing about $1,000 damage.

The school filed vandalism charges against the boy the following day. Two weeks later, the district held a multi-disciplinary team meeting at which the boy was certified as disabled.

An administrative law judge agreed with the boy's parents that filing the juvenile court petition had violated IDEA, because it could be considered a change of education placement. But the school district resisted the law judge's order to dismiss the juvenile court charges.

Under IDEA, schools must obtain parents' consent before changing a student's placement for more than 10 days. If the parents object, IDEA directs that the student "stay put" until a hearing officer or court resolves the dispute.

In the Tennessee case, the court said the school's action could have resulted in the student being placed in a juvenile detention home, which would be a change of placement.

The Sixth Circuit said a multi-disciplinary team, including the parents, must review "all decisions which seek to initiate a change in placement" of students who are disabled or are in the process of being certified as such.

"By filing a juvenile court petition, the Knox County School System threatened Chris with a fundamental alteration in his educational program," the panel said. "The school system's filing of the petition is at odds with its obligation to provide Chris with a free and appropriate education under the IDEA."

The court said school officials conceded that one purpose of filing the petition was to "secure rehabilitative services" for the student.

Under IDEA, the court said, "the school system must adopt its own plan and institute a [team] meeting before initiating a juvenile court petition for this purpose."

Congress's 1997 rewrite of IDEA generally allows schools to suspend disabled students if they act violently or bring weapons to school, but for no more than 10 days. Any longer suspension requires that school districts continue to provide education services in an alternate setting.

HOW TO USE POLICE PROCEDURES

Writing Security Policies and Procedures: Balance and Common Sense Are Key

As incidents of school violence become more common, so do board policies addressing the problem — as both a way to deal with the problem and a way to stave off lawsuits.

But how much can you really "legislate" safety? And what, specifically, should policies say?

Two schools of thought exist. The first, says National Alliance for Safe School Executive Director Peter Blauvelt, prefers policies that lay out strict guidelines. When students commit an offense, administrators want to look at a policy and read exactly what action to take. The opposing side allows for a broader interpretation, giving administrators discretion in doling out punishments.

"There are administrators who say they need options, and there are administrators who say, 'Just tell me what to do and I'll do it,'" he says. "Somewhere between the two is the appropriate mix."

Zero Tolerance

Perhaps nowhere is the need for balance more publicized than with zero tolerance.

The way many zero tolerance policies are written gives educators no options when dealing with kids, says Blauvelt. The result is a litany of news stories about students suspended and, in some cases, recommended for expulsion, for fighting, sharing over-the-counter drugs or candy, or possession of toy and/or lookalike weapons.

"One of the problems with board policy is that it become political. Everyone wants strict rules, and boards end up catering to voters' pressure by saying, 'Look, we have zero tolerance policies.' But no one ever looks at what the policy is really accomplishing or asking whether the school is safer because of it," he says.

Policies are most effective when they define an offense using language in state laws. Blauvelt asks, "What is the definition of a knife in [your state]? If you incorporate that language into the policy, you have some guidance to follow and a credible leg to stand on. If you don't, the policy is too vague. A big pen could be used as a weapon. Are you going to suspend a kid for bringing a big pen to school?"

"It's like we keep getting hit over the head with a 'stupid stick,'" he says. "There has to be room for common sense, room for educator assessment."

A well-designed policy gives administrators the authority to take appropriate actions "when, in the opinion of that person, the child presents a clear and present danger to himself or to others," says Blauvelt. "Much board policy-writing is going overboard. There's too much reliance on the written word and not enough attention to the players involved."

Policies vs. Procedures

Rather than concentrating on security policies that, according to Blauvelt tell readers only "what they can do, not what they can't do," schools should focus on developing thorough safety and security procedures that explain point-by-point for principals and staff what to do when confronted with a problem.

"Some schools think that by passing another policy they'll take care of behavioral problems. But there are some things you can't write a policy about," he says.

Some of those things include what to do if confronted by a stranger in the hallway or if a student defiantly calls a staff member a name. These situations should be detailed in a procedure guide, preferably in a small pocket size for all staff.

This makes the policies and procedures easily accessible and, he adds, "it takes the guesswork out of [dealing with situations]."

After development, all procedures should be presented during staff development time to ensure everyone is familiar with them.

—April Moore

To Search or Not to Search — And How to Do It

Security Director Offers Practical Advice for Searching Students, Bookbags, and Lockers

The bus driver says he saw a student put a knife in his bookbag. Two students say they saw a gun in a classmate's locker. One student accuses another of stealing something during a class.

These are just three of thousands of situations that raise a timeless question: When and how should students be searched? The 1985 U.S. Supreme Court decision in T.L.O. v. New Jersey attracted substantial attention to the subject. But a number of lower court decisions this year indicate that school leaders still act in ways that raise contention.

Reasonable Suspicion

Joe Harrell, director of security at the Charlotte-Mecklenburg (N.C.) Schools, emphasizes that all searches must be reasonable. "That's the big word — what's reasonable to a prudent person. If it doesn't feel reasonable, don't do it."

Case law says that in order to search a student, school personnel must have "reasonable suspicion." That is, principals can search when a prudent person in the same situation also would believe a search to be appropriate.

One of the criteria for establishing "reasonableness," says Harrell, is direct observation. A principal who encounters a student smelling of marijuana and exhibiting slurred speech and glazed eyes, for example, would have grounds to search the student for drugs.

Another relatively clear-cut standard of reasonableness is a report of contraband by another adult. If a bus driver reported that he or she saw a student put a knife in a bookbag, and the only place the student has gone is from the bus to school, then the principal could search, says Harrell. The action would stand up because it was based on "adult suspicion."

Student Accusations

Because they're in a better position to know what their peers are doing, students provide administrators most search tips. But school officials must weigh these carefully, says Harrell, since student accusations can be motivated by jealousy, vengeance, and other emotions as readily as by actual offenses.

"With students' observations, you've got to consider the source to a much greater degree. If the student is known to faculty for not telling the truth, then you need to develop another layer of suspicion. If the reporting student is known to be of good character, the accusation is going to carry more weight and there's no need," he says.

Expanding the witness list is the easiest way to cultivate a basis for a reasonable search. Ask reporting students, "Who else saw him or her with the knife?" When more than one student gives the same story, school officials are "on much firmer ground," says Harrell.

Time and Place

Time is essential in determining "reasonableness." Searches should be carried out as soon as possible after a principal has established reasonable suspicion — not an hour later, a day later, or when it's more convenient.

"If something happened yesterday, I'd be extremely hesitant to search today," says Harrell.

Also, says Harrell, the principal or searching party should go to the student, rather than calling him or her to the office. The latter situation creates an opportunity for students to get rid of whatever contraband you anticipate finding.

All searches should be witnessed by another staff member, as well. Without a witness, no one can testify as to what you did and didn't do. And, says Harrell, whenever you search a locker or bag, you risk being accused of stealing something yourself.

Voluntary Cooperation

Before searching a student or a student's possessions, Harrell asks them if he can do so. If consent is obtained, he says, "a judge will view it as a voluntary search, not a forced, arbitrary situation where rights are violated."

Simply ask students if they would mind if you looked in their bookbags, cars, purses, or lockers. Most students won't mind, he says.

When students refuse to cooperate with a search, Harrell says the issue is forced only when there is a threat of immediate danger — such as when a student allegedly has a gun. Otherwise the student's parents are contacted, and he or she is suspended out-of-school for insubordination.

Searching a Person

Searching a student is the most risk-laden of all school searches because it is the most intrusive.

An adult witness must be present whenever a student is searched. If the administrator is of the opposite gender, then he or she needs to find two men or two women who can execute the search in a private area where the student won't be embarrassed.

Ideally, school officials will never have to touch a student. Harrell says he asks students to turn out their pockets and take off their shoes. "If you're looking for dope or for a knife, it's usually going to be in the pockets or bookbag," he says.

If you want to search something more closely, like a jacket, ask the student to hand it to you.

"I will not search a child forcefully unless I actually eyeballed a gun or knife in someone's pocket. If I have, then I'm going to proceed because it's a public safety issue and someone could be immediately injured if [the weapon] is not confiscated," says Harrell. "And in this case I'd rather be criticized later than to have a student shoot someone."

Searching Bookbags, Purses, and Lockers

Searches of personal items, such as bookbags, purses, or lockers are less intrusive because they are not part of the student's person.

When a decision is made to search a student's personal belongings, Harrell tells principals to go to the class where the student is, request that he or she come with you, and watch him or her pick up and carry the purse or bookbag in question. The principal should then escort the student to a private area where the search will be done.

Again, Harrell obtains consent by asking, "Do you mind if I look through your bookbag?" and then conducts the search with a witness present.

Searching a locker is a bit different because it is school property and, as such, can be searched by school officials at any time. Charlotte-Mecklenburg students sign waivers acknowledging awareness of this.

But, says Harrell, "I will not search a locker by myself and I will not advise anyone else to."

Searching a Vehicle

Harrell says parking lots are searched by drug dogs from the sheriff's office approximately twice a year. If a dog alerts on a vehicle, it's

Teachers Should Defer Searches to Security Staff or Administrators

Teachers are excellent witnesses and reliable information sources when determining the reasonableness of a search, says Joe Harrell, but they are best off to let principals carry out the actual search act.

"Most teachers don't know how to deal with search and seizure, so my Golden Rule is to report the problem to the principal. The principal has more experience in deciding if a search is reasonable or not," he says.

When asked about a Fourth Amendment case decided this year by the Eleventh Circuit Court of Appeals (Jenkins v. Talladega City Board of Education), in which the classroom teacher and a guidance counselor strip searched two second-grade girls when $5 was reported stolen during a class, Harrell said, "I'd tell the student she was out $5, and I never recommend strip searches."

Regarding the money, Harrell said that even if the teacher found it, most bills don't have any easily identifiable marks on them that a student could point to and say, "That's mine." "You can't really identify a $5 bill as stolen unless someone confesses to taking it. In this situation, I wouldn't push things far at all."

Items that can in some way be identified, such as calculators or Walkmans®, command more attention. "Those you can press a little further because they can be identified as one person's or another's. But it's still best for staff members to refer the situation immediately to the principal."

searched in the same way that a bookbag or purse is searched. The student is brought to the vehicle and asked to open it in front of the school principal and a witness.

If a student refuses, the school suspends his or her parking privileges. The district requires students to sign a waiver acknowledging that their cars can be searched.

Documentation

After a search, Harrell recommends that administrators document what happened, including the date, time, their rationale for initiating the search, what was or was not found, and who the witness was.

"Most principals do [a search] and are off to the next adventure," says Harrell. "But I document everything so if something comes up down the road, I have something to refer to."

For more information, contact Joe Harrell at 704/343-6030.

EFFECTIVE ZERO-TOLERANCE ENFORCEMENT

Elements of a Successful Zero Tolerance Policy

Program Elements

Using zero tolerance is far more complex than issuing a policy and expecting students to follow it. At schools where the practice has succeeded, several common elements are present.

A Clear, Specific Policy

Specify exactly what behaviors or property you intend to ban, and the consequences for ignoring the policy. Policies need to be straightforward and simple, something that students understand, something that is easily publicized, and something that does not discriminate among students.

The policy adopted in San Diego was based on California's criminal penal code, which provided well-defined criteria for violation. It also eliminated potential conflict among district constituents over what items and behaviors should be included in the policy.

Community and School District Cooperation

Effective zero tolerance involves community-wide effort; it is not a practice restricted to school district staff. Support from school board members, parents, police officers, and court officials is essential. Police officers must be willing to exercise the proper intake procedure for students who violate a zero tolerance policy; court officials must hold students in juvenile detention hall until they can be seen by a judge; and the judge must work with families to find out why students act the way they do.

Student Knowledge and Understanding of the Policy

Publicity is a key aspect of the program. Before implementing zero tolerance, students in San Diego were shown videotapes depicting weapons and behavior prohibited by the new policy. Contracts signed prior to the school year are also used to alert students and parents to their obligations under zero tolerance.

Perhaps the most effective way to publicize zero tolerance policies is enforcement. Under zero tolerance, students are sent to juvenile hall for bringing a weapon to campus.

Uniformly Applied Consequences

Effective zero tolerance means school administrators have zero discretion in applying consequences when students violate the policy. The same procedures must be followed each time a violation occurs, regardless of who is involved.

One way to encourage consistency in the intake process is to turn all

---

Zero Tolerance Gone Too Far?

The Salem, Ore., school district used a zero tolerance policy to defend its October suspension of an 8-year-old boy for singing a parody of a popular "Barney & Friends" song.

Instead of singing, "I love you, you love me, we're a happy family," Douglas Mansfield III substituted, "I hate you, you hate me, let's kill...," and listed the names of several classmates. He was referred to a counselor when one of the girls named in the song complained. He was suspended after allegedly singing the song again.

violations over to police officers. Turning violations over to the police ensures consistency, and a program will go bad without consistency.

Tips on Maintaining Public Support for Zero Tolerance

Keep drastic action within the confines of the penal code. If a weapon or incident does not meet specific criteria defined by law, it should be handled administratively as a general rules violation. Expulsions to alternative education should be reserved for only the worst offenses.

Develop an alternative education program. Students who are removed from school need an opportunity to continue their education in a structured environment. By just expelling them, the school is not really helping them, and is potentially making matters worse on the street.

Keep everyone well informed of roles within zero tolerance. School officials need to work closely with law enforcement so beat officers understand the program. The judge in the juvenile system must understand why it is more important to detain kids on zero tolerance charges than to detain kids in other situations. Reinforce to police officers the importance of arresting students.

Zero Tolerance in Practice

To illustrate the best application of a zero-tolerance policy in a noncriminal situation, National Alliance for Safe Schools director Peter Blauvelt takes a page from the year's news:

"Say you have a youngster who gives a classmate a Midol®. That's a drug, but it's not a controlled and dangerous substance, and yet under some zero tolerance policies, this student will be expelled or recommended for expulsion.

"What should happen is that the principal should hold a conference with the student's parents, in which they and the student are told that the school can't have students dispensing any medication, whether it's over-the-counter medication or not — and that it's not to be done again. If a friend has need for a Midol®, then she should see the school nurse.

"That's a fair warning. That makes common sense. If the youngster insists on doing it again, however, then it's fair to bring sanctions to bear. But the first time an offense occurs, a parent conference is really all that is needed."

Rutherford Institute Appeals Suspension Over Toy Gun

The Rutherford Institute is taking Loudoun County, Va., schools to court for suspending a fourth-grader who brought a plastic toy gun to school (January 7, 1999).

The institute claimed that school officials denied Brandon MacLean his right under state law to appeal the school board's decision to suspend him.

The nine-year-old was initially suspended for 10 days and recommended for expulsion after a classmate told school officials that she saw him with a BB gun as they walked home from school. School officials said they were compelled to expel MacLean by a 1995 state law banning all weapons, including toy guns, in schools.

Ultimately, they reduced his punishment to a two-day suspension, arguing that although the toy gun he carried in his book bag was inoperable, he displayed it in a threatening manner.

Needless Suffering?

"School officials are so determined to enforce zero tolerance for weapons that they won't even pause to reflect before causing a child with a harmless toy to suffer needlessly," said Jean-Marc Gadoury, spokesman for the Charlottesville-based Rutherford Institute, a conservative civil liberties group.

Virginia, like other states, strengthened rules against carrying weapons in schools in response the federal Gun-Free School Zone Act of 1994. The law encouraged states to ban weapons from school property or face losing federal funding.

Many states now mandate severe penalties for bringing a gun, real or toy, to school, according to Julie Underwood, general counsel for the National School Boards Association.

Nearly all school districts ban firearms, real and imitation, according to figures released from the National Center for Education Statistics.

Virginia, like other states, gives local school officials some flexibility to tailor punishments for specific cases, but suspension or expulsion is usually mandated, Underwood said.

Part IV

Internet and WWW Guide

Safer Schools: A Web Sites Guide

"**Early Warning, Timely Response,**" a guide jointly developed by the U.S. Education and Justice Departments and released after last year's rash of school shootings, helps school administrators, parents, community members and others identify early indicators of troubling and potentially dangerous student behavior. The guide includes sections on: characteristics of safe schools; early warning signs; getting help for troubled children; developing a prevention and response plan; responding to crises; and information on further resources.

Available online at *http://www.ed.gov/offices/OSERS/OSEP/ earlywrn.html.*

"**Creating Safe and Drug-Free Schools: An Action Guide,**" an earlier guide from the Education and Justice Departments, gives school officials and community members step-by-step help in implementing safe-school precautions, including how to get parents and teachers involved and formulating contingency plans.

Available online at *http://www.ed.gov/offices/OESE/ACTGUID/ index.html.*

Also visit the Safe and Drug-Free Schools program Web site, which contains information on model programs and school safety grants, at *http://www.ed.gov/offices/OESE/SDFS.*

The Center for the Prevention of School Violence at North Carolina State University, has identified a "safe schools pyramid" that sets forth the elements needed for safe schools. Established in 1993, the center seeks to create environments in which students can learn and that empower students themselves to address the problems which exist in their own schools. The center sees school resource officers as integral to an organized approach to tackling school crime and violence. It also issues newsletters, research reports, and public service messages.

Visit the center online at *http://www.ncsu.edu/cpsv/.*

The National School Safety Center at Pepperdine University, established by President Reagan in 1984, seeks to train educators, law enforcement officers and community members to identify the warning signs of potentially dangerous students and help educators share resources in fighting school violence. The center also issues many school safety publications and offers both onsite technical assistance to schools and school inspections. They compile school violence statistics and have a quick-reference "checklist for characteristics of violent youth." In addition, the center serves as a clearinghouse for current information on school safety issues and maintains a resource center with more than 50,000 articles, publications and films.

Visit the center online at *http://www.nssc1.org/home.htm.*

The National Alliance of Safe Schools, founded in 1977 by school security officers, is a nonprofit research, training and technical assistance organization dedicated to ensuring students attend schools in an orderly and secure environment. NASS helps school administrators evaluate their schools for safety, avoid costly hardware "fixes" that don't solve the real problems, and base decisions on accurate information instead of "rumor and innuendo." The alliance also holds workshops so educators can improve their crisis plans, investigative techniques, and even their survival skills.

Visit the group online at *http://www.safeschools.org.*

The National Association of School Resource Officers represents more than 3,000 school-based law enforcement officers and school administrators. The association serves as the largest training organization for school-based police and district personnel in the nation, and sponsors an annual school safety training conference each summer as well as regional training sessions.

Visit the group online at *http://www.nasro.org.*

Also visit **The National Association of School Safety and Law Enforcement Officers**, a similar group of school safety professionals, at *http://www.nassleo.org.*

The "Keep Schools Safe" Web site, a project of the National School Boards Association and the National Association of Attorneys General, offers a 10-point plan for making schools safer as well as case studies of successful safe schools and information on how parents can get involved.

Visit the site online at *http://www.keepschoolssafe.org.*

The Safe Schools Hotline, sponsored by Crisis Management Communications Network, provides a secure point on the Web for teachers, parents, students, and others to anonymously report suspicious behavior. The hotline is a needed service, in the words of CEO James Gaskell, since "in almost all incidents of school violence, it is definitive that persons, sometimes several, have knowledge of the incident before it occurs."

For more information about subscribing to the hotline, call 800/496-9000.

Visit the hotline's Web site at *http://www.safeschoolshotline.com.*

National School Safety and Security Services is a Cleveland-based consulting firm that helps schools prevent and manage violence, reduce risks and liability, and improve public relations. It's services include school security training, school safety planning, crisis preparedness, gang awareness, and security assessments, along with practical strategies to address threats such as bombs and bomb threats, drug abuse and sales, concealed weapons possession, gangs, computer offenses, student threats, juvenile crime, violence prevention, and related school safety issues. The firm's inhouse book, **Practical School Security: Basic Guidelines for Safe and Secure Schools**, is available at online booksellers, including Barnesandnoble.com and Amazon.com.

Visit the firm online at *http://www.schoolsecurity.org.*

Did You Know?

Only 25 states have statewide initiatives that address the varied aspects of school crime, from prevention to crisis management, according to Pam Riley of the North Carolina Center for the Prevention of School Violence.

"We need every school in every state to have school safety plans that include prevention, intervention, and crisis response," Riley said.

Part V

Financial Support

Government Offers Grants to Halt School Violence

Three federal agencies launched a $180 million program on April 13, 1999, to help some districts run far-reaching school safety programs, hoping to help educators prevent violence rather than react to it.

The federal Safe Schools, Healthy Students Initiative (SSHSI) will provide funds for up to 50 local education agencies to hire school-based police officers, purchase security equipment and run safety-related education programs, such as after-school activities, truancy prevention programs, and mental health services.

Lawmakers authorized and funded the new program last year and the Clinton administration hopes Congress will provide $300 million total over three years.

Participating districts will have a great deal of latitude to spend the funds, federal officials have emphasized. Districts could run alternative education programs, start teen courts, or pursue conflict-resolution initiatives.

Helping, Not Punishing

Attorney General Janet Reno emphasized the need to provide mental health services to students, one of the activities required under SSHSI.

"We need the medical community to address some of the mental health issues that may precipitate violence," Reno said. Otherwise, schools and society in general will pay the price.

How to Apply

To qualify, districts first must demonstrate in one consolidated application to the Departments of Education, Justice and Health and Human Services that they have developed a six-point, community-wide plan for improving student health and safety.

The plans must be developed in "formal partnership" between districts, local law enforcement agencies and local mental health providers, and with collaboration from families and community-based groups.

To be considered comprehensive, safe-schools applications must describe how districts would improve safety in the school environment, mitigate student alcohol and drug abuse, and incorporate safety procedures into larger school reform programs.

Additionally, the Education Department says districts must demonstrate a need for federal help and describe the mental health services — referral, treatment, and follow-up — they will offer to children and youth.

Federal officials encourage administrators interested in SSHSI to obtain a copy of the Education Department's 1998 report on school safety, which includes a chapter on designing research-based violence prevention programs.

- *Applications to the Safe Schools, Healthy Students Initiative are on the Internet. See www.ojjdp.ncjrs.org, www.SAMSHA.gov or www.ed.gov/offices/OESE/SDFS. Fax-on-demand is available at 800-638-8736.*
- *The "1998 Annual Report On School Safety" is free from ED Pubs, P.O. Box 1398, Jessup, MD 20794-1398; 877/4ED-PUBS; fax 301/470-1244; Internet, www.ed.gov/pubs/AnnSchoolRept98/index.html.*
- *"Early Warning, Timely Response," the Education Department's guide to safe schools, is undergoing a second printing. It is available on the Internet at www.air-dc.org/cecp/guide/pdf.htm.*

Safe Schools Companion Initiatives On Tap

The $180 million Safe Schools grant competition is one of a slew of federal grant projects that provide money to schools and school districts for violence prevention and safety initiatives (April 13, 1999).

Schools will be lead applicants under the interagency Safe Schools grant project, but they must work in close collaboration with mental health and justice agencies. Schools may contract with those agencies for needed services.

Among those providing funding opportunities is the Substance Abuse and Mental Health Service Administration (SAMHSA) under the federal Health and Human Services Department. SAMHSA will spend about $25 million on Safe Schools and another $10 million or $15 million on related activities under a broad school-violence initiative.

Under Safe Schools, SAMHSA's Center for Mental Health Services (CMHS) will fund interventions that have been empirically tested and demonstrated successfully in the fields of child development and education.

In addition, CMHS will issue a $5 million solicitation for school, community action, and piloting grants. The program will offer community groups, families, service providers, social agencies, nonprofit organizations and faith communities the opportunity to formalize their violence prevention efforts.

CMHS also wants proposals for technology innovations to develop creative alternatives to reduce violence and provide training options that can be used by students, families, educators, and community leaders.

The Education Department will provide $60 million for the competition. In addition, ED will fund new school anti-drug coordinator activities.

The Justice Department's Office of Juvenile Justice and Delinquency Prevention will provide about $15 million and Justice's COPS program will kick in additional funds.

To be eligible for funding, applicants must propose a community-wide strategy that addresses at least six general topic areas, including: drug and violence prevention and early intervention, school and community mental health prevention and intervention services, and early childhood psychosocial and emotional development programs.

Each school district must describe — in detail — a plan for identifying and serving children with mental health needs. Districts also must describe how their plans to support early childhood development services will promote safe and healthy environments in which children can live and learn.

For information about the Safe Schools Initiative, go to the Internet at http:// www.ed.gov/offices/OESE/SDFS.

Non-School Applicants Can Tap Safe Schools Opportunities

School districts are likely to be key grant recipients under the multi-agency Safe Schools Initiative (SSI, April 1999), but other organizations may have a crack at the estimated $210 million pot.

Agency officials are planning a coordinated grant program under SSI. With multi-agency funding streams, school districts could take a comprehensive approach to combating school violence.

Applicants could submit one application for funds for a variety of prevention, mental health, and other activities, says Mike English, in the Center for Mental Health Services at the Substance Abuse and Mental Health Services Administration. The budget gave SAMHSA $40 million for SSI.

If the current plan flies — it isn't final yet — additional grant opportunities are planned that schools and other applicants could tap, English says.

The current provisional scenario calls for final decisions on program direction by year's end, and if it's a go, a coordinated program announcement in the Federal Register.

But there are fundamental issues to iron out first, English emphasizes. Among them:

- Funding Mechanics — whether school districts should provide multi-year or up-front funding. Few school districts could launch comprehensive programs and effect significant change in school violence in one year. On the other hand, future funding is uncertain;
- Program Emphasis — whether the program will focus on

- **Safe Schools:** The Health and Human Services, Education and Justice Departments are inviting applications to fund safe school projects with heavy emphasis on mental health prevention and interventions.

Applicants must submit local comprehensive plans addressing six elements: creating a safe school environment; youth alcohol and drug prevention, violence prevention and early intervention; school and community mental health preventive and treatment intervention programs; early childhood psychosocial and emotional development; education reform; and safe school policies.

Deadline: June 1.

Funds: $180 million in first-year funding. The maximum award is $3 million.

Eligibility: Local education agencies, but only in partnership with local mental health and law enforcement authorities.

Contact: See these Internet sites for detailed information: http://www.mentalhealth.org; http://www.samhsa.gov; and http://www.ed.gov/offices/OESE/SDFS.

strengths of students and building healthy schools or school violence and enforcement; and

■ Other Partners — whether other agencies will join in.

Designated lead agencies are SAMHSA, the Office of Juvenile Justice and Delinquency Prevention, and the Education Department, but the Centers for Disease Control and Prevention and others have shown interest.

ED plans to contribute $10 million to the coordinated program via the Safe and Drug Free Schools program, staffers say.

Congress gave the ED program a $60 million increase for competitive national activities this year — shifting money from noncompetitive state grants — plus $35 million for a new competitive middle-school drug coordinator grants program.

Education Department to Fund School Safety Coordinators

The Education Department is inviting applications to recruit, hire, and train drug prevention and school safety program coordinators for middle schools with significant drug, discipline, and violence problems (March 1999). Coordinators will:

■ Identify research-based drug and violence prevention strategies, and help schools adopt the most successful ones;

■ Develop, conduct, and analyze assessments of school crime and drug problems;

■ Work with community organizations to ensure students' needs are met;

■ Work with parents and students to obtain information about effective programs and encourage their participation in program selection and implementation;

■ Develop evaluation strategies;

■ Identify additional funding sources for drug prevention and safety initiatives;

■ Provide feedback to state education agencies on successful programs; and

■ Coordinate with student assistance and employee assistance programs.

Deadline: July 28, 1999.

Funds: $31.7 million for 300 awards ranging from $55,000 to $106,000 a year. The project period is 36 months.

Eligibility: Local education agencies.

Contact: Ethel Jackson, Safe and Drug-Free Schools Program, 202/260-3954; www.ed.gov/OESE/SDSF.

Police Help School Agencies Hire New Campus Cops

Schools and school districts with their own police forces are in prime position to build their ranks under a Community-Oriented Policing Services (COPS) initiative funded by the Justice Department.

School districts without their own police can work in partnership with local police departments to seek assistance, says COPS spokesman Kevin Avery. Rural and other schools in communities without police departments can reach out to local sheriffs' offices and police in neighboring communities, he says.

There are caveats and requirements for all police applicants. They must:

- Assure that officers employed under the program will be assigned to work in primary or secondary schools;
- Enter into a partnership agreement with either a specific school official or with an official with general educational oversight authority in the jurisdiction;
- Document, identify, and justify problems, such as gang violence at or near schools, for example by using crime data, school surveys, or community complaints;
- Demonstrate quality and level of commitment to the program, for example, by showing evidence of previous successes and impact; and
- Provide information on how proposed activities are linked to an overall community policing strategy.

While the department has no census of how many schools have their own police, 8,000 of the 47,875 officers on the street last summer under Justice's broad universal hiring program called schools their beat.

For application and additional information on the program, contact Department of Justice Response Center, 202/307-1480, 800/421-6770; Internet, www.usdoj.gov/cops. The CFDA number is 16.710.

Notes